The Talking Stick
VOLUME 24
Undercurrents

The Talking Stick
VOLUME 24
Undercurrents

A publication of the
Jackpine Writers' Bloc, Inc.

© Copyright 2015 Jackpine Writers' Bloc, Inc.
All rights reserved by the authors.
Cover photograph by Rebecca Komppa.

Send correspondence to Jackpine Writers' Bloc, 13320 149th Avenue,
Menahga, MN 56464. sharrick1@wcta.net

ISBN: 978-1-928690-27-6

Table of Contents

Table of Contents

Table of Contents

Table of Contents

Co-Editor's Note–Sharon Harris
Editor's Choice: "Remains" by Susan Niemela Vollmer (p. 85)

Maybe I am just at a certain age and a certain time in my life, but this poem really grabbed me. How sad that the person in this poem wanted to spend forever where he was happiest but it was not to be. How sad that his loved ones perhaps did not know him well enough to know what he really wanted. Or they did not care enough. It does seem like a person's last wishes should be respected.

This year we buried my last remaining uncle, my dad's last sibling. All the older generation of his family is now gone. He chose to be in the same cemetery as my dad and mother, two rows down. Uncle had been in the army for a large part of his life. The 21 gun salute sent birds fluttering from the trees as we all shivered in the cold. Then we warmed ourselves with shots of Uncle's favorite whiskey, served on top of his casket in the cemetery. We toasted Uncle and Dad both that day, remembering their closeness, their laughter. We were glad they were close again.

Also this year, we buried the last of the old neighbors in our farming community, the last old friend of my parents. These folks broke the ground, built the barns, milked the cows, and filled the farmhouses with us, their children. When these farm families sold the cows and retired, they turned to hobbies they loved and went dancing. We, the middle-aged, their children, now take on the mantle of the oldest and wisest. We are now the elders, learning how to grieve and move on.

This makes me think of my own end. I like the romance of having my ashes spread somewhere, to float over a place that I loved. But I am kind of stuck in tradition like my parents were and know it is nice for loved ones to have a grave site to visit. I'm not sure yet, but I suppose I should be making up my mind.

What really remains of us when we are gone? Deep down, I know it does not matter if we are in a coffin or if we are ashes in an urn on a shelf or spread somewhere to float away in the wind. What matters is how we lived, who we loved, and who will remember us. We need to know we have connections to other souls; we want our stories preserved—and what better way than with the written word.

Co-Editor's Note–Tarah L. Wolff
Editor's Choice: "In the Attic" by Peggy Trojan (p. 39)

Saving things takes courage that people don't often talk about. I once held a set of dishes in an antique store that literally made my heart skip. They were an incredible deal, several full place settings for only $25. Everything about them from the ceramic they were made of, to their creamy finish with humble blue adornments. They were tough, not shiny and they had lasted many years already. They were exactly what I had always wanted and I loved them completely. I was also in a dead end relationship and still living at home with my mom.

I did not buy them.

Later my mother saw my sad face when I told her about them and she could not understand. It was so simple to me: I did not buy them because to buy them and put them away on the chance of never retrieving them would have broken my heart.

She talked of hope chests and that I certainly should gather for my hopes and future but I didn't have the courage. It seemed, with my luck, to buy something like that was putting the wagon so far out in front of the horse it would jinx me. And I flat out did not believe in buying anything unless it was useful to me right *now*.

Peggy Trojan's poem called "In the Attic" that I chose for my Editor's Choice this year touches on these things. If my own death had been as untimely as the subject of this beautiful poem I would have hated for anyone to have found, and then had to decide what to do with, my dishes that I never got to use or put in my own home.

Nowadays (only three years since I passed up those dishes) my life has changed considerably; I am now a Mrs. with a home of my own in my grandparents' 100 year old farm house after a full renovation. So now, as you might have expected, I have scoured every antique store and the internet and I cannot find them.

Perhaps my mother was right, maybe I should have bought them but maybe I was right about the jinx. Perhaps not buying those dishes that I wanted beyond reason (and suffering the disappointment of leaving them on the shelf) was exactly what I needed. It was not long after that the events began that started the chain reaction that brought me all the way here, wishing I had them to put in my home.

Judges

Poetry Judge

Laura L. Hansen graduated with a B. A. degree from Concordia College in Moorhead, MN. She worked in Administrative Management for twelve years followed by twenty years as a bookseller. Laura has two published poetry chapbooks, *Diving the Drop-Off* and *Why I Keep Rabbits,* and has been published in numerous regional literary magazines. She has won numerous L.O.M.P. awards and prizes and was chosen for the People's Choice Award in the 2013 On the Wall Contest at Q Gallery in Brainerd, MN, and was the third place winner in the 2014 contest. Her poetry has aired on Lakeland Public Television and on KAXE's "The Beat." She lives in Little Falls, MN. She loves water, her dogs, willow trees, birch trees, books, writing, and making mosaics.

Creative Nonfiction Judge

Marge Barrett, who earned an MFA in creative writing from the University of Minnesota, has published a poetry chapbook, *My Memoir Dress*, stories in Dzanc Books *Best of the Web 2009*, the Minnesota Historical Society's *The State We're In*, and poetry and prose in numerous journals. She teaches at The Loft Literary Center in Minneapolis and conducts a variety of workshops.

Fiction Judge

Mary Casanova grew up in St. Paul, MN. The family often headed up north to a cabin. These treks instilled an early love of wilderness that eventually led Mary and her husband Charlie to move to the Canadian border after college. She is the author of well over thirty books, from picture books to middle grade to YA novels. Her books frequently land on state reading lists and have earned many awards, including the ALA "Notable," *Parent's Choice* "Gold" Award, *Booklist* Editor's Choice, and two Minnesota Book Awards.

Winners

Poetry 1st Place
"On the Occasion of My Untimely Demise" by Adrian S. Potter (p. 1)

Adrian S. Potter is from Minnetonka, MN, and writes poetry and short fiction. He is the author of the fiction chapbook *Survival Notes* and winner of the 2014 Lebanon Poets' Society Free Verse Poetry Contest. Some publication credits include *Vermillion Literary Project, Kansas City Voices, burntdistrict* and *The Broken Plate.*

Creative Nonfiction 1st Place
"Terminal Burrowing" by Kristin Laurel (p. 2)

Kristin Laurel is from Waconia, MN. Her first book *Giving Them All Away* won the Sinclair Poetry Prize from Evening Street Press. She owes her passion for writing to The Loft, where she has been a student for the past eight years.

Fiction 1st Place
"Sure Shot" by Al Rieper (p. 3)

Al Rieper grew up in rural Wisconsin. He went to school there and in Minnesota and has lived in Maplewood, MN, for many years. Al writes fiction and poetry for fun, for friends and for the challenge. He enjoys meeting with other writer friends, hanging out with his adult children, travel and tennis.

2nd Place and Honorable Mention

Poetry 2nd Place:
"Broken Bowl" Cindy Fox (p. 6)

Poetry Honorable Mention:
"Her Purse" Susan McMillan (p. 37)
"Hanging On" Jan Chronister (p. 128)
"Bone" Stephanie Brown (p. 158)
"Remains" Susan Niemela Vollmer (p. 85)
"Putting Down Roots" Nicole Borg (p. 54)

Creative Nonfiction 2nd Place:
"What You Can Hear Carried on the Wind"
        Kathryn Knudson (p. 7)

Creative Nonfiction Honorable Mention:
"The Final Amen" Audrey Kletscher Helbling (p. 81)
"Buckle Up" Eric Chandler (p. 163)
"Go Gentle, Dad, into that Good Night"
        Charmaine Pappas Donovan (p. 149)

Fiction 2nd Place:
"Book by Book" Bonnie West (p. 9)

Fiction Honorable Mention:
"FAQs" Paula L. Hari (p. 97)
"Another Man's Treasure" Larry Ellingson (p. 103)
"Geraldine" Paisley Kauffmann (p. 123)

The Talking Stick
VOLUME 24
Undercurrents

Poetry 1st Place by Adrian S. Potter
On the Occasion of My Untimely Demise

Look for me at the front of the church
inside a lacquered box, synthetic smile

crafted from the corners of my mouth.
Witness me primped and shorn properly,

stuffed into a practical suit, pinstriped and
fresh-pressed. Come on inside, genuflect,

and seek silent reflection or the discomfort
of a hardwood pew. Sing a good old hymn.

Pay your respects and comfort others, even
if all you can think about is having a drink.

Afterwards, drag your ass to the corner bar
that I frequented. Chat with the bartender

who listened to the struggles of my days
as if they were fairy tales, who withstood

my whining for a better life until it became
as familiar as the creak of the front door.

Mention my name and watch her eyes alight
with memory. She'll mix up my proper eulogy

in liquid form, two parts wrong, one part right,
poured over several ice cubes, stirred gently.

Creative Nonfiction 1ˢᵗ Place by Kristin Laurel
Terminal Burrowing

Handsome Sven's on the TV, jabbering about the weather. He says it's been the coldest winter in decades, but I don't need a meteorologist to tell me that. All I have to do is take a look outside my window: You've never seen an old dog look more pitiful trying to pee fast and not sink into a six-foot snowdrift.

I've spent over half of my life in this state. Hell, even James Wright couldn't hack it. I wish he would have gotten out of Minneapolis more; he might have liked it better in Waconia. Out here, there's hot coffee and doughnuts at every gas station to Ortonville. Out here, there's a community of ice houses on every frozen lake. Even though there's more drinking than writing poetry in there, you have to admire the occupants for being creative.

I should hate it here but I don't. It's true. I haven't seen a neighbor in months, but at the grocery store a tall grey-bearded man with a staff in his hand held the door open. He looked so wise and reminded me of Gandalf (except for the purple Vikings sweatshirt). His lips were dry and cracked and even though it must have hurt, he smiled. Meanwhile, over in the produce section I overheard a young woman say, "It sure is cold, but at least the sun is shining." And then I heard another woman with the voice of my grandma say, "Today's the kind of day to stay home and make soup."

I let the dog back in, shut the TV off and warm up my soup. I wrap myself up in my blanket and sink into the couch. I pick up a magazine and find an article about hypothermia. It says that in the final stages, humans have been known to dig themselves into a hole and die. It's called "terminal burrowing" and it has something to do with the brainstem shutting down. Well now, that's one hell of a metaphor. That explains everything.

Fiction 1ˢᵗ Place by Al Rieper
Sure Shot

Max's eyes blurred and he edged the barrel of his rifle off the stumpy fence post. He ducked down into the tall grass and pulled a shirt tail out of his jeans to wipe his eyes. "Think, moron," he muttered. "You got plenty of time." In a couple more minutes, the tractor would make the turn at the end of the field bringing his target even closer.

Who the hell am I talking to? "Nobody," Max answered himself aloud. "And you'd better get used to it." After this, who would there be to talk to? They'd have to send him to jail, wouldn't they? There'd be no more high school buddies to run with on the weekends, no girls on the bus to tease or laugh at his jokes, no brothers or sisters, no mom there to listen or understand why. Not where he was going. Could there even be other sixteen-year-old guys in prison? Probably some big city prison, he guessed, maybe way down by Minneapolis or St. Paul.

With clearer eyes, he looked for the John Deere and its driver at the end of the field. It wasn't like anyone could blame him, not after they heard all the shit his old man had pulled for years. Of course, who would believe it? Hell, Jack, Jenny and all his other brothers and his sisters knew it, had lived it every day. They'd secretly bow down and thank him. In her heart, his mom probably would too. She'd finally be free. And safe. Somebody had to rid the world of this twisted bastard before the day he finally went too far.

That day was bound to be soon. A river of reasons flowed through Max's mind. Like last fall when the chainsaw bucked back into his leg. He was bleeding all over the woods and the floor of the truck, but his father wouldn't take him to town for stitches 'til the day's work was done. Or this winter when the old man had broken Frank's arm with a pitchfork handle and then made fun of him for putting his arm out "to save his ass from a lickin' he damn well deserved" for spilling a whole pail of milk. And especially because of a month ago when Jenny walked in from the barn just in time to see their dad pinning Mom up against the milk house wall with his hands around her throat.

Max grabbed his cuff, pulling the left pants leg up as if to show. To show who? Anyway, his leg scar had faded quite a bit. The others were just in his head. But yeah, he was the oldest boy, a man almost. It was up to Max or the old man probably would kill one of them first. *A judge might listen*, he reasoned. *It's self defense right?* His mom could tell in court just like she'd told Max last night, about yesterday when she'd come home from her Ladies Aid church meeting and found the old man sitting at the table red-faced, temper boiling, holding a loaded shotgun and about how she had bolted screaming back down the driveway. What was her loving husband's excuse? He'd yelled after her, "Honey come back, it's not what you think. I'm not gonna hurt you. I was waiting for Max." *Yeah, that was a lot better. He wouldn't shoot his wife, just his son.*

Today Max was the one waiting. The putt-putt of the tractor came closer now and he turned the deer rifle toward the sound. Not daring to fully stand, he ground his knees into dirt and pebbles, resting the barrel of the gun on the second lowest strand of barbed wire. A slight slip sideways over one of those barbs brought blood trickling down Max's left wrist through a sheen of sweat. Still, he felt nothing, saw nothing but a live target atop the approaching green tractor. The boy wished he had a scope to help him get a really sure shot. This had to be a head shot, so he wouldn't have to go into the field to finish the job. Max had killed animals before. He sure didn't want to hear any groaning or pleading, didn't want to have to see the damage close up.

Shit, that wire made a shaky rifle rest. Not good enough, but by also bracing the gun against the side of the fencepost and squinting through the sight, he slowly drew a pretty good bead. The hat, the head, his dad's sunburned neck, all were in easy range, as Max's finger rested lightly in place, but by then the tractor had passed. *Not in the back, that wouldn't be right*, Max thought. *Let him take one more trip around. One more pass will make it just right.*

Ten minutes later the sight line was true. The old man had even eased off the gas, lifted his straw hat and begun mopping sweat with a kerchief, as he looked back at the plow, admiring the dark furrows stretched out in the soil behind him. Perfect. That bald head

4

was shining in the sun for the last time. *Just squeeze one off. Don't jerk,* Max cautioned himself.

As Max's finger curled around the trigger, the old man looked skyward. A single bird soaring overhead had caught the old man's eye. When he looked up, so did Max—hoping for a crow, some specter of death, some "go ahead" sign. But this bird was much bigger, lighter colored than a crow, probably a hawk. The old man rose from the tractor seat laughing. He waved his hat, whooping. "Whooping at a damn bird," Max mumbled. "The nearsighted fool probably thinks it's an eagle." He always whooped just like that on the Fridays after cashing *his* milk checks, laughing and bragging, "The eagle shits gold on Friday," about *his* payout from *all of their* work. Max's finger fell from the trigger guard, and he eased the gun barrel down off the wire, down into the grass.

He hated his old man, but he had to admit liking one part of him—that laugh. Pure bullshit of course, but people said it sounded a lot like Max's. In the next endless moment, he didn't decide *not ever* to shoot his old man. But as Max licked the salty red stream running from his wrist and forearm, as he slowly slipped the rifle back into its case, the boy knew it wouldn't be that day.

Max crouched low, dodging cow pies, making his way back beyond the tree line. As he circled through the woods toward the barn, he was frowning. His limbs were shaking and he was muttering to himself again but not hearing, not seeing. Sweat and tears stained his favorite T-shirt. His jeans were torn at the knees and soaked at the crotch. But Max knew one thing. It would have been a sure shot. Fifty yards into the trees, when he came to a familiar, gnarled oak with a face that Max knew appeared only to him, he stopped to breathe.

Once again he unsheathed the rifle. He leveled it at the face and said, "I'm not going to jail today. Not for you, you sick bastard, not on a Friday." Max pulled the trigger, sending one round through the oak's bark and deep into the trunk, right between two knotholes.

Poetry 2nd Place Cindy Fox
Broken Bowl

I broke my mother's big bowl today, the largest one of a four-piece set she gave me for a wedding present. The bowl that fit in the crook of my arm like a baby, whipping up birthday cakes and pancake batter. The bowl that felt tiny fingers mix their first batch of Rice Krispie bars, scraping and licking the sticky goodness. The bowl that held comfort foods—mashed potatoes or round steak that had simmered in gravy all day. The big bowl that survived five house moves, packed in old newspapers with the smaller bowls safely tucked inside. The bowl that outlasted my marriage and now, forty-four years later, slipped from my dishwater fingers and shattered in the kitchen sink. I tenderly wrap the broken shards in yesterday's newspaper, slip them into an empty cereal box so the sharp edges don't tear the garbage bag and the pain is so deep it's like losing my mother all over again.

Creative Nonfiction 2nd Place by Kathryn Knudson
What You Can Hear Carried on the Wind

Where I'm from there was no mythology, just rich black earth and gentle rises and tenuous proximity to an area Laura Ingalls mentioned briefly. Laura's fleeting stopover was miles and miles from where my family lived but felt closer in experience—for us, too, Mankato was a bustling destination. When her cascade of books eventually branched to a television show, a generation of girls wore braids, wishing they also drank cold water out of ladles and rode in covered wagons through a southern Minnesota they didn't know looked suspiciously like southern California.

We had only the normal, the mundane: evenly-spaced towns strung together on a railway line; two Lutheran churches for fewer than three hundred people; men playing dice at the restaurant and cards in the back of the grocery store, across the hall from a butcher chopping apart a quarter beef steer.

For a time, while she was in high school, my mother was that butcher, her first job there in the back of Kenny's store. If you ever think you have a tough mom, just think of one who'd used a cleaver at seventeen. Now Kenny's is a ghost fingerprint on a lot recently reclaimed and landscaped after decades of being saddled with farm machinery, but when I was young the store was going strong. I remember walking slowly up the steps, through the screen door. The aisles' wood floors warped familiarly with age as plastic wrap and toys and pie pans sat next to Kool-Aid and Velveeta and all the other foods that made the '70s fairly glow with unhealthiness.

Kenny was always there, half glasses resting on his nose or hanging from a chain and, if he hadn't scared me just a tiny bit, he would have blended in my memory with Mr. Hooper, the grocer on *Sesame Street* whose death was the first my friends and I cried over. As it was, Kenny stands out in my mind, tall (to a kid's frame of reference, I imagine) and opinionated and intelligent and patient while I laboriously counted coins from my palm onto the counter for a

Jolly Rancher sour apple stick or a bag of flour, depending if the errand was self-driven or directed by my grandmother.

After she moved back with a master's degree and well-used passport to marry my father, my mother and Kenny met regularly for coffee over at the restaurant. Their discussions often turned into debates which just as often devolved into arguments; in the years she was away, Kenny had become much more religious, now believing a narrow, literal reading of the Bible. He was so conservative my Peace Corps-volunteer mother nearly cried with frustration. There were times she returned home to slam the cupboard doors, rattling the plates as they stood, driving us to our rooms where we stayed as quiet as possible until the storm passed. Mom and Kenny fought and talked and laughed, coffee after coffee, year over year, until Kenny's body, well-eaten by cancer, was buried in our church cemetery.

Grief and pain and loss wrap around, terrifying in their ability to cut us off from one other. *Sesame Street* had not prepared me for this; seeing my mother's sadness up close mystified me. She explained, as best she could, what it felt to lose a friend, a mentor, someone who'd given her her first paying job. Kenny had believed she could become a butcher who could go to college, who could go on to impact people's lives. He encouraged her to think, to stand up for herself, to fight for her beliefs. She'd loved Kenny. "No, not at all like I love your dad." She laughed genuinely when I asked. "A different kind. The love of a friend who knows you well and loves you back in spite of. Or possibly because."

Back then, she learned to have faith in herself, the sound of playing cards slapping across the hallway, the screen door banging from the traffic of customers, and the cleaver slamming down, a rhythm carried on the prairie wind until it became a whisper. Where I'm from there is no mythology. No fables. Just memories and recollections like that of an insecure farm girl who found herself standing unsure at a butcher's block, eventually understanding what a few others already knew, that she was much stronger than she could imagine.

8

Fiction 2*nd* Place by Bonnie West
Book by Book

V ictoria combs the stacks for books. She's searching for her story. She likes using the library. She hates the computer, calls it *the machine* much to the annoyance of her husband who is on his all the time. The days of card catalogues—lovely wooden cases with index cards in long, long drawers—are over. She wonders if she could still get her hands on one.

She loves books, actual books and thinks their days too, are numbered.

She's looking for stories about affairs. She did first try the computer, searched the word "affair" on Google, but was inundated by all the things she didn't want:

Struggling with Infidelity? affairrecovery.com. If you have betrayed or been betrayed we invite you to take this simple and free assessment. Affairs Club Dating—Local wives looking for a discreet affair. www.affairsclub. Free! Affairs Chocolate & Desserts www.affairs-chocolate.com.

Also of course, she found gruesome retribution sites and shocking pornography. She knows she'll get spam for months to come.

Even with the library's computer system of cataloguing books there's no certainty under *Subject* the affair will be listed if it's secondary to the story. She found one illicit love story in a book on the shelf whose description was *dogs, men and lost civilizations.*

Victoria has been in the Nokomis Library by her home, and others across town, volunteering and reading about affairs for nearly a year. While she sorts and re-shelves books, she hunts for the stories.

An elderly man's casual lover dies. He's never met her husband during the years of the affair. After her death he's struck with a strange curiosity about him. At the wake he introduces himself and is embarrassed by the gratitude enthusiastically expressed to him for coming. He realizes the enormity of her husband's grief, so much so that he is overwhelmed by grief and guilt himself and confesses.

In fiction adulterers are always found out. In real life she knows it isn't true.

She spends countless hours in the libraries searching book by book for her story.

A receptionist whose lover is also her boss learns of his death when she arrives for work one morning. Two years later, still despondent, she learns his home is for sale and cannot deny her urge to attend the open house. While pretending to be an interested buyer she's confronted not only by him in countless family photos but also by his sweet wife who, in a strange plot twist, tearfully confides that after her husband's death she discovered he'd had ongoing affairs with numerous women.

At the James J. Hill Library in downtown St. Paul, Victoria reads a poem in which two young lovers commit suicide rather than be parted. She surprisingly feels such sorrow she sits at the heavy wooden table and cries.

Her lover is ten years older than she; her husband is four years her junior. She believes no one would ever suspect a woman of trading in a robust young man for an older one. It has given her an odd sense of safety.

Her husband is never particularly curious about her, where she goes or what she does, so her affair continues undetected. She and her lover believe at first, the affair might burn itself out but *the flames grew higher*—words from a silly country western song her lover sings to her in bed. He's a great fan of Bruce Springsteen, can recite the words to all his songs. He referred to Springsteen as The Boss. One evening on the nightly news, she discovers it's what the whole world calls him. The news anchor wishes The Boss a happy fortieth birthday and she's shocked to suddenly hear the song she and her lover have made *their* song: *the sheets soaking wet . . . a freight train running through the middle of his head . . . bad desire*. She's massaging oil into her husband's feet, something she has done weekly for ten years.

She and her husband never planned on having children and they didn't. They relished being free to travel, to own two homes and a boat, to come and go as they please. Her lover is divorced with four sons and three grandchildren. She thinks they take advantage of him.

Two lovers see each other for several months. In love they believe themselves to be soul mates. The man decides to leave his wife and intends to marry his lover. After one steamy afternoon he calls to check in with his office and is told by his secretary his wife has been trying desperately to reach him because their daughter has been in an accident and is in critical condition. He rushes to the hospital but it's too late. His daughter dies twenty minutes before his arrival. He never sees his lover again as he cannot bear even the thought of her.

Victoria doesn't know what her husband would do if he found out about her affair but she suspects having an affair would be seen by him as less a crime than having it in a seedy motel.

Her lover is a co-pilot for a small commuter airline. The first few times they were together, she offered to pay for better rooms but he wouldn't hear of it. She admires him for that.

Once at a party she began discussing aircraft maintenance horrors. When her husband glanced curiously at her, she said she'd read it in a magazine adding, "Roger, over and out," shrugging as if she really didn't know what she was talking about.

She never tells anyone about her lover.

The library books are her only confidants. She nods and smiles while reading, discovering what she recognizes intimately: longing, desperation, indecision; wishing to stay and go at the same time, to suspend time, to speed up time, to know the outcome. In her heart she knows she won't know the outcome until it is upon her.

She can't decide what to do and is searching for the answer. She wants no one hurt, least of all herself.

Every story she reads has a different twist but mostly they end badly.

The evening of their wedding anniversary, her husband comes home with a lovely wine: Cote de Beaune, Grand Cru Burgundy. As he's decanting it in the kitchen he tells her he thinks it will be more fun to stay home with a good wine and some delicious stinky French *fromage* than to go out.

She carries the plate of cheese to the coffee table and he follows with two crystal goblets of wine. He sits next to her on the couch and passes one to her.

"Cheers," he says.

"Cheers." They clink glasses and she takes a sip. The wine is off. *Corked*, she thinks. It has a bitter stale taste.

A man fixes his wife her morning cup of tea. He's found out recently she has a lover but doesn't want to confront her for fear she might leave him and disgrace him in front of his colleagues. He decides to kill her by slowly poisoning her. He frets over her and gently nurses her so she never suspects. During what might be her last few days, her lover arrives at the apartment and tries to see her. A fight between her lover and her husband ensues and her husband is accidentally killed. She survives since the poisoning has stopped, but her husband is dead and her lover has run away. She never learns she was being poisoned by her husband and without that knowledge realizes how much she loved him after all.

Victoria watches her husband carefully spread the triangle of the cheese onto a chunk of baguette and start to chew. Then he lifts his glass, gives her a big grin and washes it down with a gulp of wine.

"Good?" she asks.

"It's perfect. Happy Anniversary."

She leans forward, thinks *this is how it ends*, and picks up her glass.

Poetry by Mary A. Conrad
on the edge

this place
of little space
I own
suggests some action

to walk along
alone
advises traction

and balance

to chance
a glance beyond
below
commends some caution

perhaps

to look
not leap
suggests some fear
or common sense

or maybe not

to leap
not look
suggests some gain
or awful loss

or both

to hesitate
or leap

to look
or lose

these are the questions

I own this edge
I choose

Poetry by Tarah L. Wolff
Shuffling

And my arguments to keep sane
slip and slip
and slip
as time presents itself as
a table
a flat surface where
all that I did
all that I will do
is pressed, coming and coming
with me in the middle
at five thousand degrees
with the weight of
compression to produce
a table
a mirrored surface
both hitting each side
of my head
locomotives that
push and push
and push
to produce a double sided
coin
my coin
where there is no
I did or
I will do
as time presents itself as
a table
a copper surface with me in
the center listening
to the shuffling
sound as fleshless
fingers casually
sort
my deck

Creative Nonfiction by Ryan M. Neely
The Fear that Fills Me

I have an unhealthy relationship with fear. It's like a marriage. I feed it and argue with it. I fight against and then snuggle close and wrap myself in it like a shield, begging it to protect me from the world. Unlike most marriages, however, I can't remember our anniversary. I don't know the exact date I chose to turn to fear and let it control me, often times against my better judgment. I just know it wasn't always like this.

I used to be brave or perhaps I was stupid (they do say the two are not mutually exclusive). My time in junior high school—the seventh grade, more than the eighth—stands out brighter and clearer in my memory for bravery. Sometimes I wish I could pull his strength into me. He was a boy who didn't take shit. He didn't care what you thought, about him or anything else for that matter. He did what he wanted to do, and if you didn't like it, well, too bad.

The feeling I get most from those days was one of righteousness. He was a boy who told you if he thought we were wrong. He'd tell you right to your face as blunt as a hammer. Maybe those days were just the beginnings of the rebellious nature I donned later in life, or maybe they were the stark contrast of the prudish nature of my seventh grade English teacher, Missus Carver.

My one friend in her class, Sean Collins, and I were the only kids heavy into fantasy and science fiction. Sean had a group of "other" friends he played Dungeons and Dragons with. I wasn't allowed to hang out with that group. My father was afraid they would lead me down a path to devil worship and we'd all rampage the town on some Satan-fueled killing spree. In class, however, Sean and I were inseparable.

We were both wicked smart, too, and most of what Missus Carver had to teach us were things we already knew, or concepts we absorbed like sponges (we were still youth back then). Needless to say, we had a lot of down time in class (which infuriated good ol'

Carver to no end) and, to occupy ourselves, we created a little fantasy creature called Fuzzball which we took to drawing on a sheet of paper we shared back and forth, the way girls in the fifties used to pass notes.

Fuzzball was cute, in my opinion. He stood all of two-feet tall and was covered with fur. His back was covered with quills, like a porcupine, and he had a tail ending in a spike. He stood on his hind legs and walked like a human, only his legs were too far apart and he was a bit wide, so we imagined he waddled. His feet were like those of a chicken, with three long toes in front and one sharp talon in back. He had large extraterrestrial eyes and a pig's snout, and fangs like you wouldn't believe dripping acid-like poison onto the floor.

As would be expected, Carver found our drawing—and in my possession, no less. Interestingly (at least to me), she seemed more upset about what she called the "demonic" drawing than the fact we were doing it in her class. I was sent to the principal's office and my parents were called. Carver accused me point blank, in front of the principal and my parents, of worshiping Satan and demanded I be expelled.

It wasn't the principal or my parents who stood up for me in the face of her oppressive tyranny. I did. The fourteen-year-old boy I sometimes wish was still around. I met the fear in her eyes and told her she was a small-minded fool who was afraid of a child's drawing. Were we worshiping Satan? Of course not. We were creating a fantasy world to take us away from the hate and fear of the world we lived in.

I wasn't punished for my drawing, or for standing my ground. Nor was I removed from a class which would cause a combative nature over the next year-and-a-half, which was no doubt the reason I followed through with my next act of defiance.

Near the end of the year we had a large assignment where we were to choose a topic or theme and collect poetry from the school's library fitting said theme. We were to write an essay about how the poems fit the theme and what they meant to us on a personal level, and then we were to stand before the class and read our poems aloud.

My topic was anonymous authors, at least on paper. I scoured

16

the school's library for all of the anonymous poems out there, and found a common secondary theme among most of them. It seemed a great majority of them were quite sexual in nature. This became a secondary theme for my assignment. One I did not mention to Carver.

On presentation day, I stood before my fellow classmates and read my selected poems aloud. One was entitled "My Pussy" and was a thinly veiled innuendo about a cat, and how the author liked to stroke it. One was titled "I Like to Touch Myself" and was less thinly veiled.

When I approached Carver for my grade, she handed me a giant red F and asked, "Was it worth it?"

"Absolutely," I said with a grin on my face and the laughter of the class behind me. The fourteen-year-old me fought that grade, too, arguing he had fulfilled the parameters of the assignment regardless of content.

Carver was forced to reconsider and I received a B+ for my anonymous poetry.

I still don't know what happened to the boy who used to live inside me. He's traded brashness for consideration, passion for apathy, and courage for fear. He's still there, deep within me, urging me to thumb my nose at authority, but he's been suppressed by the fear of said authority.

I hope one day he comes back and we can divorce the fear that fills me.

Poetry by Ronald j. Palmer
When I was a Child

I was afraid of bees
of being stung
as once I was

what did I know
of the search for nectar,
the opening
of petals,

or the coming
of the fruit

now, I am glad
when the bumble
buzzes by, knowing

an awakening is near.

Poetry by Peter William Stein
Lotus Born

At any moment, my breath
could heal me completely
if I would only take notice,
instead I suffocate in the salty sea
to search for the ancient architecture
of a lavish civilization

On occasion, I emerge
to transcend the surface
like a lotus blossom,
open effortlessly
in the clear light of air

The want of all
the hidden city has to offer
returns, so I submerge
to struggle against the current,
seek the empty treasure chest
and forget the cleansing breath

Poetry by Nicole Borg
Signs

One road leads to another
or leads away from roads
I might have taken, had I known.
But Grandfather's compass is broken
or north has shifted by degrees.

That map in my chest,
the one that speaks
in Grandmother's voice,
is calling out directions.
My mesmerized feet follow,
kicking up dirt and dreams.

There is no moral to this story,
at least not in the way
my parents let me believe.
I'm always searching for signs—
a crow's feather flashing
blue in the sun, wind parting
the flax in a confiding way,
dreams I forget upon waking
that ease into my thoughts
        and quickly out.

Fiction by Kathleen Lindstrom
Blue Schwinn Bike

He comes home every day at this time. I watch him park in the alley, get out of the car, reach in the back seat to pull out his lunchbox and jacket, maybe the morning paper, maybe a bag of groceries he picked up on the way home. He carries them up the sidewalk—a tall, thin guy with graying hair, dressed in a navy blue shirt, dark gray pants and clunky brown boots.

He is stooped and slow, as if dragging three-hundred pounds behind him. I see scuff marks on his boots, dirt on his pants, stains on his shirt. He emits a stale odor—like dried sweat, or maybe the smell of a hard day's work. I wait on the back stoop to welcome him home. When he sees me, he tries to smile, but the smile takes forever, or too much energy. He tousles my hair, which I pretend not to like. "Hello, Squirt," he says, opening the squeaky screen door behind me and disappearing into the house.

I hear them in the kitchen, saying the same thing every night. "How was your day?" "Fine. How was yours?" "Fine." Sometimes he'll kiss her on the cheek. Sometimes he'll pinch her on the butt. I hear the clatter of his lunchbox as he places it on the counter, then the rustle of a grocery bag, then the clack-and-whoosh of a beer being opened. I hear him drop into a kitchen chair with a sigh. I hear him take off his boots, and two *thuds* as they fall to the floor.

I hear her call my name: "Betty Marie Martin, get in here and set this table." But I take my time, picking at the scab on my knee, watching it bleed. An ant runs across my bare foot, hurrying home to a mound of sand built between two slabs of stone. I think about squishing it but don't.

I go inside and let the screen door slam, which makes her flinch. She's wearing a dress with tiny purple flowers. Her yellow apron has ruffles, a big bow tied in back. She stirs something on the stove (macaroni and cheese tonight) and he sits at the table, drinking his beer, watching her, waiting for something to happen. I never know

21

what.

Sometimes it's hard to breathe in here.

I slap down the plates and silverware and she turns to give me the *look*—slits for eyes, fangs for teeth. *Can't you be more careful? More ladylike?* I give her *my* stare and she shakes her head in disgust, returning to her pots and pans. I purse my lips, all prim and proper now, my pinky finger pointing to the sky, *daintily* laying down a fork, then a knife, then a spoon, mimicking her perfect Ladyship. I look at him, feeling hilarious, wanting him to share in my joke.

But he's not in his chair. He's standing behind her, by the stove, his arm around her waist nuzzling her neck, mumbling some words. She shrugs him off, annoyed, too busy for such nonsense. So he falls back down into his chair, sighs, stares at the big yellow bow, looking sad. I want to make him smile. So I reach out and touch his hand. But he jerks away, as if stung by a bee.

He leaves the room and heads for the bathroom where I hear him pee, flush the toilet, run the water.

We live on Jefferson Street at the top of a steep hill where neighborhood kids come to ride their bikes. I sit on our front porch, watching them hike up the hill, leaning into the wind, gasping for breath as they reach the top, then mounting their bikes (all smiles and wild eyes) then pushing off and barreling down past our house, their legs spread wide, screaming all the way.

I wonder what such daring feels like.

The macaroni and cheese is hot and I spit it out while she stands behind me, pouring milk into my glass. I hear her *tsk.* It makes me smile. I keep hitting the table leg with my foot, trying to find some rhythm, trying to pound some noise into this place. But she turns and gives me the *look* again—all slits and fangs, thunder and lightning. I take my time. I'm not hungry. The air is thick with fog, blurring edges, muffling sound. My heart is pounding; my stomach hurts.

He is buttering his bread while we watch Walter Cronkite on the news. But the butter is hard and rips his Wonder bread to shreds.

22

He doesn't notice. Walter is excited about the men who landed on the moon. "It's a new era," Walter says, eyes wide with the wonder of it all. "The world has changed. Anything is possible now."

I don't know what he means . . . but then maybe I do.

I watch him watch the news for a while, and then I don't. Instead, I'm at the top of the hill on the Schwinn bike I'll get some day, which is light blue, with a white basket and red tassels. I pedal to the edge, close my eyes and let the hill take me down. I am an eagle, fierce and keen, plunging off a mighty mountain, held up in a pale blue sky, afraid of nothing. I soar past everyone else and am first to reach the bottom of the hill.

He looks up. He is impressed.

* * *

Poetry by Angela Ahlgren
After the Gray

I know you're not
supposed to look
directly into the sun

but today I let my eyes
open wide to its light,

a black pine skeleton
twig-thin against its glow
and beyond that,

blue times infinity.

Poetry by Patrick Cabello Hansel
No Eulogy

My father should not have died.
He should not have given his last breath
as a whisper no one could hear. I should
be able to call him tonight after the sun
is down and talk about the best ways
to can late-season tomatoes. We would bemoan
the Vikings, joke, catch up on my siblings,
pray—more with a fist than a bended knee—
that the blood the Republicans wrested
from the nation will soon clot, darken, begin
to attract brighter wasps. I don't know who
I am writing this to. I would claim heaven
and earth for witness, but they have hidden,
each behind the other. My father would smile
somehow, through the telephone lines, say
"I love you, too," hang up the phone;
float for a moment—his voice, his fire on the air—
like all dead fathers. I do not want
that. I want the live one back. The voice
roaring, the breath unshackled. I want
the nearly full moon outside to be his word
and the planet I see—tell me, Father, is it Jupiter
or Venus or Mars—to be the space between
our words, a light travelling from sun
to planet to earth. Three lights, three beings.
Father. Son. Nothing. The nothing that calls,
that moves in the night, in the body,
when hope feels like surrender.

Poetry by Chet Corey
The Huddle

Rain warping its awning
down like a body bag
being hefted to a gurney,

a handful of its "regulars"
huddled beneath—
their faces menus of grief.

The sign on the cafe's
entry door says, "Closed.
Beloved Owner Died."

The rain thundering down
on the awning like
applause at a Springsteen

concert in East Rutherford,
for another, another
and yet one more encore.

Poetry by Mary Jones
Silence

Since he died, she can't abide the
silence of the empty house. She fills it up
with noise, talking heads on CNN,
dancing celebs on ABC, genteel
aristocrats on PBS. She turns the
stereo on full blast—Bach, Beethoven,
Brahms.

She doesn't
understand this since he never talked
much and the house was silent
even when he was alive. She finds it hard to eat
her solitary dinner at the kitchen table with
his empty place mat staring at her,
accusing her of what? She never cooks
anymore. What's the point of
cooking just for one?

And so
she gobbles down frozen dinners
in front of the TV, in front of
the latest breaking news, wars,
shootings, bombings, tornados.
Victims and survivors talk about
how it feels to go on in the face of
such tragedy, how they will pick up
the pieces of their lives.

She too has been
through the war, is both victim
and survivor. But no one asks how
she will cope. There is no drama here,
just the silence,
the silence and the empty house.

Creative Nonfiction by Larry Ellingson
Memorial Day

The veteran's cemetery was about an hour away and they gave me a couple of adult diapers, just in case. Sure enough, we only got a few miles when his bowels gave way and a sour stench filled the car. I pulled off onto a side road and got him into a clean diaper. His pants were soiled and we didn't have a clean pair, so I rolled them up and put them in the trunk. We turned around and went back so that I could clean him up and make a fresh start.

We were making our way up the ramp to the group home when Dad spotted a crew of men working on the road. He was unaware that he had no pants. I saw him stop and look at the men and I knew something was coming. Dad had been in the Army Corps of Engineers. He worked on the ALCAN highway during World War II and built roads and airfields in Korea. He drove bulldozers and operated cranes; and he told other men what to do. So when he stopped on the ramp and I saw his eyes narrow and focus on the men, he was back there. He drew his lower lip into his teeth and let out a loud whistle, like he used to do when he wanted to get someone's attention. The men stopped digging and looked at this big old guy in a diaper. "Come on Dad, let's go," I said. He slowly focused on me and we started back up the ramp. The men went back to their work.

We gave him a quick shower, got him into clean clothes and started out again. I put in a CD of old standards and he looked out the window and whistled along with some of the tunes. The veteran's cemetery was filling up fast when we arrived. We had to park on the road, nearly a quarter mile from the entrance. Golf carts were picking up old veterans and shuttling them toward the entrance. I hailed one down and helped Dad into it. The cemetery is 100 acres of awe. It has a pond and a fountain and numbered rows of graves and a "garden" for urns. There are simple granite monuments to the missing and to the fallen of past and present wars. There is a central square with the U.S. flag on the tallest mast surrounded by flags representing each branch of service. They had set up a large open tent with a stage and row upon row of metal chairs. We got seated and Dad looked around, admiring the landscaped grounds, the sidewalks curving away from the square and the solemn, stately slabs of granite. His hands resting on his lap moved back and forth as if working the levers on his bulldozer as he shaped the mounds, sculpted the earth and moved the rocks into place.

The local high school band started playing and the honor guard brought in the flag. Everyone sang the national anthem. Then each generation was recognized for their service. I rose for Vietnam and other men and women, impossibly young, stood for the Gulf war and Iraq and Afghanistan. The commander of the National Guard wanted to give special recognition to the World War II vets, to pay homage to the sacrifices made by them and their families. "That's you, Dad," I said when he asked them to rise. I helped him get to his feet, shaking, unsteady, but determined to stand. He rose to his six foot three height and squared his shoulders. He looked around at the handful of other veterans from his time, maybe looking for familiar faces, those grinning, dirty, exhausted, frightened and exuberant young faces he had known. Those who came home merged into their communities and rebuilt a nation reeling from a Great Depression and a second Great War. Now they were dying by the hundreds each day, regiments of them, marching to the graveyards, casualties of time.

When the speeches were over and the crowd began to disperse, we visited Mom's grave. It was hard to believe that it had been two years already. We looked at the space reserved beside her and I followed his gaze up and down the row of headstones. Afterwards I suggested that we go into town for a drink. To hell with the clinics and the hospitals and their safe and fussy advice. We found the American Legion club and I asked for two glasses of their best Scotch, make it doubles. Dad had always liked a good Scotch. I watched as he tipped his glass and held it to his lips and tasted the sweet, sharp whiskey on his tongue. He smiled and we clinked our glasses together and I felt warm and numb at the same time.

"How about a Dairy Queen?" Dad suggested on the way

back to the group home. I remembered how those words excited us when we were kids and he was the driver. It was a rare treat and my sisters and I bounced up and down on the back seat that was as wide and soft as an old sofa. We would arrive home with chocolate faces and sticky hands. Mom and Dad would line us up and scrub us clean with a warm washcloth. "Good idea," I said. We stopped and got two chocolate-dipped cones and sat in the car eating them. I turned to face him and he grinned at me, ice cream dripping down his chin and onto his shirt. I reached for a napkin and wiped his chin and dabbed his shirt. "Thanks, son." Thank you, Dad.

* * *

Poetry by Mary Schmidt
Sorbet

Sun scoops orange sorbet
on a melting warm twilight
blue sky licks it up.

Poetry by Frances Ann Crowley
In October

the quaking aspens are busy forecasting.
All dressed up in shivering gold and sun-made glitter,
they stand in one straight line and whisper.

What are they saying as they chatter and shiver, wave and
         shimmer?
Has one seen a wooly bear caterpillar with a narrow brown stripe?
Did another see pigs gathering sticks or geese and monarchs
skipping town earlier than usual?
These are signs of a harsh winter or so says
the old farmer in the almanac.

We cannot know their thoughts. We are not fluent in aspen.
We can only savor their honey-gold and the crisp apple air,
knowing that winter, be it harsh or mild, creeps around our edges.
We quake and tremble.

Fiction by Niomi Rohn Phillips
Family Secrets

Charlie hesitated at the door to the visitors' lounge. He realized that after twenty years the shroud on one of the best-kept family secrets was about to be snatched away.

When Lee Graham phoned him at the University, Charlie assumed the unknown caller was a solicitor of some kind. He was abrupt, anxious to get off the phone.

Then Graham said, "My dad just died. We found some letters among his papers in a lock box that concern you."

"What's this about?"

"I'd like to talk to you in person. It's taken months of detective work to track you down. I could be in Fargo next week. I could meet you at your dormitory."

For years Charlie had replayed childhood memories for clues: Grandma bursting into the room where he was sitting on the floor rocking himself after they took Mama away; Grandma talking loud and sounding angry, pulling clothes from dresser drawers and snatching up dirty clothes from the piles scattered on the floor; Grandpa putting him and the suitcase in the car.

After a long ride, they got to a small town and Grandma and Grandpa's house. Grandma tied an apron around her waist and bustled around the kitchen. Grandpa took a fishing rod out of a hall closet and said, "Let's go to the river."

Charlie learned quickly that Grandma was firm and in charge and expected unquestioning obedience. But she always came into her sewing room where he slept on the spare bed to tuck the goose-down quilt around him and say "*gud nacht*." And once when he had a cold and his eyes were stuck shut with goop in the morning, she sat on his bed and gently wiped his eyes with a warm, wet washcloth.

His mother wasn't there for a long time. "She's in the hospital," Grandma said when he asked. And he overheard words like "nervous breakdown" and "shock treatments" when Grandma

31

talked to Aunt Katherine. They didn't want the neighbors to gossip, but he knew they were talking about his mom when he walked into the room and heard "*sie ist . . .*" and "*er ist . . .*" Grandma spoke German for things that were none of a kid's business, like when Grandpa came home from the tavern, late for supper, walking carefully, one foot in front of the other. She would lead him from the kitchen door to the bedroom spewing German all the way. Charlie stayed put. Grandpa was a big man. One of these days he might just turn around and smack her. But he never did.

And Grandpa could be counted on for quiet, contented hours on the river. Just the whirr of the reel as the line arced overhead and into the water. No need to talk.

Charlie stayed with Grandma and Grandpa in Bergdorf off and on for a couple years. A neighbor in the city apartments where he and Mama lived would call when Mama got sick, and Grandma and Grandpa would come to get him. The car was heavy with Grandma's glum silence on those trips. Grandpa would look straight ahead, concentrating on his driving, and then take their fishing rods out of the hall closet when they got to the house.

In third grade Charlie and Mama moved in with Grandma and Grandpa permanently. Mama worked in the potato fields in the spring and fall and tended bar on Saturday dance nights at Schwaan's tavern. Any job she could find in that small prairie town, he realized later.

He had cousins who lived on a farm, and Grandma and Grandpa and even Mama thought spending time at the farm was a treat for him. He hated all of it—calf riding, jumping in the hay mow, his skin itching later for hours, crawling into the granary door and climbing the hill of grain that could come rolling down like an ocean wave and bury you.

"Sissy. Wimp," his cousins taunted and tattled. "Charlie's afraid of everything."

"Must take after his dad," Uncle Nick would snort.

The one time Charlie got up the courage to ask about his dad, Grandma said, "He's dead," in an Amen tone boding no further discussion. He never brought it up again. Kids are smart that way. It was like knowing not to make the sign of the cross at your Protestant friend's dinner table, and not tell your Catholic Grandma you went to

Wednesday night Bible School at the Baptist church.

Protestants were on the bottom of the social scale, but a notch above Charlie. He was marked. Grandpa bought him a Schwinn bike for his ninth birthday, so he could ride with the other boys, but they usually left him far behind in the dust of the gravel roads.

In school he kept his hands to himself and his eyes on his work—that was the mantra of the nuns. He didn't want to risk getting the swat of a ruler or a pinched ear. Most of the nuns in their sweeping black gowns and clicking rosary beads scared him, but when they appreciated him with compliments about his reading or his math, it just made his life harder.

"Teacher's pet," he heard at recess.

He never forgot the day a snowball broke his glasses, stumbling home, stomach churning with worry. He knew glasses were very expensive.

He did come to understand that the shame clinging to him wasn't only his mother's embarrassing sickness that they couldn't talk about. Grandma called it "her weakness" or "female trouble." But Mama wasn't married when he was born. He asked her what it meant just once after he heard "bastard" at school recess.

"We were young, I got pregnant, he left, end of story," she said. "There's nothing else to tell."

There were lots of things you didn't talk about in the 1950s, weaknesses like depression and having a baby out of wedlock. His mom wasn't a single parent; she was an unwed mother.

One day near the end of his junior year in high school, Sister Dominic asked him to stay after class. "Your grades are good enough to get a tuition scholarship at the State University," she said. "I know someone who can give you a job on campus. You can work for your room and board."

Charlie found his place at the University. He had friends. No one cared about his past.

And when he walked into the visitor's lounge at Sayre Hall, he knew he was about to find some answers about his dad. Looking at Lee Graham was like looking in a mirror.

Poetry by Sharon Harris
Let Me Show You Something

Step off the safe sidewalk with me
to a spot you haven't seen.
this side of town is silent
and drugged and dreary
and I never linger long.

walk with me by this wide, slow stream.
the water is thick and heavy
and slaps against the shore.
let the movement enter your veins.
smell the water, thick and heavy as it passes,
hear the damp things growing.
envision what may reside on this river's bed,
lost and long forgotten.

see how a fish flings itself into the air
and how the water bends and curves around it
even after it is gone, back below the surface.
imagine the water closing over you,
lapping a last time against your face
as you sink to the bottom.

see how the moon reaches down
and dips a long finger into the froth
for a taste.

Poetry by Kristin Laurel
Pedaling

I like to be alone with other people
on our bikes we are all alone
pedaling around this City of Lakes
and even though I'm pedaling, my thoughts are still spreading
out like ants on a checkered blanket
where a family is having a picnic
eating processed food
drinking corn syrup from plastic bottles
which will harden their arteries.
I worry the bottle may end
up in a landfill for centuries, or out
in the Pacific, waiting to be swallowed by a whale,

the last whale, who may become extinct. But,
there are still sunfish today
and out on the dock, children are fishing,
red and white bobbers bobbing, lapping it up, with the e-coli
and all of the other hidden
dangers of the world.
I cannot worry about the soul of a sunfish.
I will try to pretend a Styrofoam cup is a toy boat.
Maybe milfoil is edible, healthy like spinach.

We are all pedaling
not braking for grief
not diving into the waves,
by the sign: CAUTION DEEP WATER DROP OFF.
The lady in front of me
has her iPod in her ears
snaps her fingers with her right hand
while her left hand holds the handlebar
her strong perfume smells like Obsession

> > >

and I pedal around the circle over and
over as the water mirrors the backdrop of our city.
"On your left," I yell, as I pass the kid
who wears a T-shirt RELIGION IS A LIE.
On the corner of Lakewood cemetery
someone has taped up JESUS SAVES.
Maybe he does, maybe he doesn't.
I'm just here for the ride today
and I'm pedaling as fast as I can.

Poetry Honorable Mention by Susan McMillan
Her Purse

In a family of eight
of shared bedrooms, one bath,
everything else sacrificed
for husband or child,
Mom's purse was her place.
Sacred. The one thing
she had to herself.

If she said, *It's in my purse,*
you did not look
but waited for her to retrieve it.
In the car if she said, *Hold my purse,*
she meant you should sit still,
its onerous weight on your thighs;
heaven help you
if it should unzip or gape open,
lest your glimpse trespass
on secrets stowed inside.

Days after her funeral, after
interment up at Hillcrest,
someone had to look.
Dad couldn't. So we four sisters
shared this desecration
as item by item her personal bits
were spread out on the table.

> > >

It was nothing. Cigarettes,
coin bag clutching a fistful of change,
note pad, ink pen, packet of mints . . .
ordinary things we'd often seen
in her hands one at a time,
but never all in one place.

I thought of feathers
out on the grass
after the goose had been eaten.

Poetry Editor's Choice by Peggy Trojan
In the Attic
For Kelley

We cleaned out the attic
at your folks', decades after
your untimely death.
Found the box of Barbies
and all their clothes:
coats and dresses
and the bridal gown.
You had packed them
with dreams
of moving on to your own
fairy tales.

They smelled musty.
In an attempt to preserve
what you chose to save,
I washed and ironed them today,
marveling at the tiny sleeves,
the little turned collars.
Then, packed them up again,
carefully, with some
old dreams of my own.

Poetry by Anne Morgan
Thaw

At three a.m., through the bathroom window,
In the eggshell glow of the outdoor light,
My backyard resembles a continent
Viewed from thirty thousand feet.

Thigh-high snow looks flat
Except for the concrete walk,
Which is being slowly reclaimed

By shovel, salt, and spring.
Wide by the house, the grey-black path
Narrows from a short, mighty river

To a compact tributary that
Branches into abbreviated streams,
Writhing like runaway snakes,
Draining winter from my world.

Creative Nonfiction by Mike Lein
Winter Life

Summer—pack a swim suit, an extra pair of shorts, and maybe a spare T-shirt. Drive north on smooth dry roads and arrive at the cabin with no more worries than how high the grass is or if the loons will yodel. The fridge is stocked, the pantry is full, and it's still light outside. A frosty mug of beer on the deck is the first order of business. That's summer. That's simple.

Now for a winter reality check. On a mid-winter weekend visit, the warm clothes for ice fishing, skiing, and trips to the outhouse take up an entire oversized duffel bag. Spouse Marcie and I head north in the dark, on icy roads with the truck packed with clothes and provisions, trusting that neighbor Bill has plowed the 1,000 foot driveway. The pantry shelves will be bare, the fridge unplugged, and any water that was left behind will be frozen as solid as Crooked Lake. That's winter. It's complicated.

Four miles north of the last small town, the road changes from civilized tar to primitive country gravel. The dark forest closes, a tunnel of snow-cloaked trees creating a Halloween spook house atmosphere. Lucky for us, the driveway is plowed. The single set of narrow tire tracks marring today's dusting of fresh snow confirms that neighbor Marv has made a security check in his old jeep. The truck's headlights swing into the cabin's yard, revealing a maze of more tracks—rabbits, squirrels, and tree-eating deer have been out scrounging in the cold.

Time of arrival is 7:00 P.M. The thermometer on the snow-covered deck reads a minus 10 degrees. The deck gets a quick shoveling so we can open the door and shuffle the first load of supplies and clothes into the cabin. Kal, the big tough hunting dog, cowers in the truck, hiding her sensitive Labrador ears from the low battery squeak of the smoke detectors. Murri, the fluffy white terrier/poodle mix, scampers through the door, eager to find a warm spot. It's a balmy 20 degrees above inside.

While I trek in more supplies and coax Kal from the truck, Marcie cranks the electric space heaters to "High" and huddles up on the couch with a blanket, the little dog, and the newspapers. It's time to catch up with the local news while the heaters do their work. The local police report, always written in a deadpan straight-faced "just the facts, ma'am" style, is full of the usual reports of road-killed deer, cattle on the loose, and fish house robberies. There's also the usual head scratchers. Why does someone call 911 because people are walking down the road, talking, and wearing glasses? Or report "gun shots heard in the forest" during hunting season?

A couple sheets of crumpled newspaper, kindling, and a big match yield a roaring fire and serious heat in the wood stove. I sit in front of it, savoring the warmth, still clad in coat, hat, and boots. Kal grabs a stick of kindling and climbs into my lap, littering the floor with chips and splinters while chewing off nervous energy.

8:00 P.M.—11 below outside, 28 above inside. The thermometers indicate an inside warming trend despite the reverse outside. With that established, the outhouse path needs shoveling, the door unlocked and the TP situation checked. Sometimes, someone forgets outhouse etiquette and leaves a roll exposed. The outhouse mouse has his way with it, shredding and scattering pieces in a frenzy of fun. And yes, there is a mouse in the outhouse.

9:00 P.M.—minus 13 below outside, 45 above inside. Even without a thermometer, the 45 degree threshold is easy to see. The snow tracked in while unloading melts on the stairs and into the rugs. I work magic with the small wood stove, playing the air flow through the damper, watching the flames dance behind the glass door while squeezing out every possible BTU.

10:00 P.M.—minus 16 outside, 55 above inside. We watch the late news and talk shows, recording temperate readings in the cabin journal to impress summer readers.

11:00 P.M.—minus 17 outside, 60 inside. Time to step outside for a last look at the night sky. Sometimes the northern lights play psychedelic tricks, changing colors and shapes while they dance around the Big Dipper. Other nights Orion blazes on the southern horizon in the midst of a thousand other stars. Tonight the full moon overrides all these, beaming down from above and ensnaring the cabin in a creepy web of tree branch moon shadows. The lake talks in muffled groans and thumps, adding its own bit of creepy.

Back inside, Kal curls up in her old overstuffed chair, saving energy. She knows there's a long list of tasks to complete tomorrow. Sipping coffee while watching the shadows of the pine-covered islands slide back across the lake towards the sunrise. Pulling on the old snowmobile's starter rope, swearing until it starts. Drilling holes in the lake and hoping the northern pike are hungry. Refilling bird feeders after the squirrels stuff themselves. Hauling firewood from the stacks behind the outhouse. Cross country skiing on the lake. Maybe even a late campfire under the moon and stars at 10 below.

While I was out star gazing, Marcie folded down the sofa bed. She's an undefined lump huddled on the far side against the wall, semi-recognizable by the Icelandic wool stocking hat peeking out. It's a scene from a modern day *The Night before Christmas.* I flip the blankets back and start to hop in to share some body heat before a long winter's nap. Murri is already there, hidden under the covers and snuggling in my spot. She utters a low protective growl and makes no effort to move. Yes, it's winter, and nothing is simple.

Poetry by Susan McMillan
After

In April
after forever cold winter
after usual breakfast of gruel and toast
in stocking feet he wanders out
coffee in hand
through the patio door
across weathered wood of a deck
that needs power wash and stain,
up concrete steps dry now finally
after layer
on layer
on layer
of ice and melt.

He stands at the corner of morning
sucks in cold air as his wide cup
steams over its brim,
looks out over acreage
that wants pruning,
over back of a house that needs
new siding. In ten quick minutes
he has to leave for work—
the day
after day
after day job
that no longer excites or rewards—
tells himself, *Only a few more years.*

Poetry by Richard Fenton Sederstrom
Glare

Waves slip and clip by us
in a tempo of marimbas.
The breeze picks up,
thirsting for waves.
Waves slurp at the sky.

Waves slap, a madness—
the insane flapping
of thick loons in thin air—
like mine, the wrong element.

The waves peck and slurp
at surface prey, which
has all died out this late
in an exhausted leaf-fall.
Prey cowers below the waves.

A surge below drives waves
sky-ward—toward the lake-
devouring haze of sun.
Below, fish devour each other.

The waves gentle our still boat
northwards, toward
the chill glimmer and weave
of ultimate borealis, the rare
visible music of night.

Poetry by Shasha C. Porter
Timing

She slides the belt through the loops of his so perfectly draped pants,
>Configures the buckle,
Scooches on the socks.
>The left foot. The right.
Labeled insignia stitched into the cashmere ribbed patterning.
>Wriggles on the shoes.
The right foot. The left.
>Italian leather, ties looped loosely.
Snugging the laces.
>Crisscrossing—
Right over left. Left over right.
>Places designer pants cuffs over the polished shoes. Just right,
While late afternoon light skims horizontally, scattering silkily onto
>the polished floorboards.
>His face *that close* to the skin of her cheek.
Eyebrows pulled down, gaze intent: The zip. The snap. The tie.
>*Such beautiful clothing*, she thinks. *Such a gorgeous physique.*
She looks up at him.
>*That dimple. That smile.*
If she'd met him sooner, before it all began, would she know how to
>navigate this,
>Without leaving?
She scoops up the coins spilled onto the dresser,
>Skitters them into his right-side pocket,
Slips her hand into his left-side pocket, fingers finding the pills:
>The small yellow, the two oval whites, the one tiny blue, the
>green . . .
To calm the body's involuntary tremors—the ravaging this disease
>brings to his being,
>The intimacy this ravaging brings,
The closest sacred space of it.

46

Poetry by Sonja Kosler
Not Here

Mother at thirty-two leans across the front porch rail.
Montana cabin air suffused in bull pine and sage.
Her left hand smoothes yellow flowered shirt over bulging abdomen
where a foot, an elbow, a hand roll from within.

She sees her daughter's future—away from here,
grown and content in a there space.

Mother at ninety-seven leans across my back porch rail,
lake ripples against shore
carries scents of balsam, of fish.

Her right hand clutches
mine for balance
here in this space of there.

Poetry by Marlene Mattila Stoehr
The Memory Tin

The button tin, who knows how long ago,
held a five-pound Hostess fruit cake.
Today, in the assorted glitter and practicality within,
I find reminders of a woman, insignificant by worldly standards,
who lived in three centuries, buffered by a courageous spirit
that carried her through 105 years.

We visited often in the 34 years we were neighbors,
frequently found her surrounded by sewing supplies,
the button tin beside her.
She might be recycling jet-black buttons on a suit,
metal crowned-eagle buttons on a coat,
or sewing pearl-button eyes on catnip mice
for her daughter's cat menagerie.

She was hesitant to reveal details of her life
yet we came to recognize the humiliation
at becoming a teen bride on her 16th birthday,
and a mother the day after.
We sensed the difficulty of life with a dominating husband,
her sorrow at being all but abandoned by this only child who,
secretly pregnant with Flora's twin granddaughters,
fled with her lover after a vicious confrontation with her father.

We perceived, bit by bit, the bitterness and heartbreak
she and her daughter caused each other.
Both now are dead, cut loose from a dysfunctional relationship
like buttons and buckles snipped from discarded clothing.
Both come alive again when I hold Flora's button tin.

Fiction by Deb Schlueter
Cabin

The car's tires crunched on the gravel road. Thick, dark forest gave way to a clearing with a cabin tucked inside. The sunset cast long shadows up the forgotten yard, encompassing the tiny building.

It had been one of the first cabins built in the area. Although it used to be a jewel, now only squirrels, mice, and the occasional skunk called it home. Covered in gray and deteriorating siding, with windows that no longer kept out the wind and a sloped and scratched floor, it looked ready to be torn down.

Behind the cabin stretched tall red pines, a few stumpy white pines, and the brambles of an old garden. Just visible through the trees lay what passed for a lake; spring reeds, mosquitoes, frogs, and ducks crowded the shore. It was picturesque—and quiet.

"Come along, Mary."

Mary smoothed the wrinkles from her skirt as she got out of the car and followed her mother up the worn path to the front door. Dressed in slim designer clothing with not a hair out of place, the woman's imposing figure stood in stark contrast to the weed-filled flowerbeds surrounding the old cabin.

Her mother stopped, eying the rotting front steps with distrust. "I'm not sure it's safe to go in."

Mary stood there a moment, chewing on her lip and playing with the key her Grandmother had left her. Then, she carefully navigated the steps in her heels, fit the key into the rusted lock, and pushed open the cabin door. The inside reeked of disuse and animal feces—not the smell her Grandmother's stories had evoked.

The inside of the cabin was one large room. Bunk beds with hand-made quilts stood along one wall, a small old-fashioned stove along another, and a wood fireplace on a third. Thick wooden planks made up the floor and walls—dusty pictures of her grandparents and her mother as a child hung precariously on nails here and there. Mary could picture this place as a paradise.

"This place is *disgusting*," her mother commented, wrinkling her nose as she made her way into the cabin. The floorboards protested under their weight. "It's falling apart." She brushed a spider web out of her face.

Mary wandered around the small room, surveying the damage caused by forty years of neglect. The mattresses were destroyed; the dishes old, but usable. The chimney would need to be cleaned. They'd need to add plumbing and electrical. She touched a rocking chair roughly made from tree branches. Her mother had spent her first few years being rocked to sleep in this very chair, before the demands of life had pulled her grandparents to jobs in the city.

"We won't get much for it—"

Mary looked at her mother. "I'm not selling it."

"What are you going to do with an old cabin?" The woman blinked, her expression a mix of surprise and distaste.

Mary shrugged. "Grandma left it to me."

"The money from this could pay for the rest of your college, get you started on a nice place in the city."

"Or I could come live here." Mary tucked a strand of hair behind her ear and grinned. "I'm almost done with college, and there's a bunch of towns nearby—I can get a job in—" She stopped at the astonished look on her mother's face. "What?"

"You can't be serious. You have a *law degree*. You've never lived anywhere but a city. Look at this place!" She gestured at the dirty, decrepit cabin. "Your grandmother left this to you so you could sell the land and make a better life, not trap yourself in the woods."

"It's been in our family since it was built. I'm not giving it to someone else." Walking over to a window, Mary peered out the dirty window at the lake. The remains of a dock and a forgotten rowboat lay on the shore. She turned quickly, almost upsetting her grandmother's old washbasin. "I'll finish college, and I'll use the money Grandma left me to fix this place up, and—"

Her mother cut her off. "No. This is insanity." Mary saw the gleam of anger in her eye. "My daughter is *not* going to live in a cabin in the middle of nowhere by herself."

"Rodney could come live with me."

"*Rodney?* You're still dating that young man?" Mary winced at the dangerous tone in her mother's voice. "I suppose he's still a writer."

"Yes, Mom." Unable to look her mother in the eye, Mary turned to the cabinets and started opening drawers. Something moved in the first one, vanishing in a flash of fur and scaly tail.

"He makes no money. He can't support you."

Mary sighed. "He doesn't have to, you know. I'll have a job, and—"

Her mother's arms crossed firmly over her chest. "*And* you'll waste all the opportunities your father and I have given you on a fallen-down *hovel* in the wilds of Minnesota and a man whose greatest dream in life is to write a book that nobody will read."

Mary's cheeks reddened as she muttered, "I'd read it."

"No. This isn't happening; I will not allow it." Her mother's brown eyes were sharp. "We are going to sell this place, and you are going to graduate next month, and get a job in a city, and a nice apartment, and meet a *decent* young man with a *future*."

"Mom, I'm twenty-four—"

Her mother cut her off with scowl and a quick motion of her hands. "I will be in the car, Mary. Get this nonsense out of your head."

Mary glared at the floor as her mother spun on her heel and stalked out of the room. As the sound of her heels retreated, Mary's fingers tightened around the edge of the wooden countertop. She waited for the door to squeak-slam shut behind her mother before looking up.

The spring sunset filtered through the dirty windows. Dust floated in the air, disturbed by their movements. Something rustled through old leaves. In this light, the fireplace looked warm and inviting.

Mary pushed away from the counter and walked back to the rocking chair. She brushed at the worst of the dust and dirt, then settled into it and rocked. It made a soothing, creaking noise.

Mary had grown up listening to her grandmother tell her about this cabin and these woods. Hunting and fishing and sewing and cooking and preserving food. Life here had always been something that captured Mary's imagination—especially when her actual existence had consisted of little more than concrete, steel, glass, and expectations.

After a long few minutes, she got up and walked out of the cabin, locking the door behind her. Weaving her way up the dirt path to the waiting car, Mary stopped and looked back. The sunset stained the cabin red.

"Let's go, then," her mother said when Mary got into the passenger side of the car. "I'm sure the realtor is still open. We can get this place listed . . ."

Mary stopped listening to her mother and pulled out her cell phone. She snapped a picture of the cabin just before the car pulled back onto the road. A few taps on the screen brought up her boyfriend's number. *"Wanna live here?"* she typed, hitting the send button.

"With you?" came the reply.

"Yeah."

"Then definitely. When do we move?"

With a grin, Mary stashed the phone back into a pocket and turned to watch the trees pass by on the road as the world darkened—pines and birches and oak trees. Her breath caught as she glimpsed an owl swooping through a clearing in search of a meal. The last of the sun faded from the horizon and already it felt like home.

Poetry by Sharon Harris
Old House

I began life
as a small square two-story house
and a root cellar basement
on this farm of hills and hollows.
I breathed and lived
and sheltered several families
through a century of seasons.

for many months now
I have waited and watched
feeling only loneliness and loss
and suffocating stillness inside me.

finally, slowly,
I begin to breathe again.
rooms move,
walls change within me.
I feel new supports, new nails,
new strength;
doorways widen
and stairs climb in new directions.
I feel the motion,
the welcome shifts in energy.

some of my eyes have closed
but new eyes are opened
to new visions, new scenes
I feel new life, new love—
flowing in
to fill my spaces.

Poetry Honorable Mention by Nicole Borg
Putting Down Roots
for Dag and Diedre

I don't recognize any of the flowers—
the prairie grass looks just like the fields
in North Dakota where I was born.
On the bluff today, there is no wind.
Anonymous plants
reach onto the walking path
to brush against me,
the enigma.

Everyone here, I say, should wear a name tag,
first and last, and carry a copy of his family tree.
In the sandy soil of this river valley,
I never know how the pieces fit, twining branches
and overlapping roots, cousins everywhere.

Ten years is nothing to prairie grass
but it's the longest I've stayed.
At least I can tell a maple from an oak—
a Meyer from a Roemer. Until my children
are grown and marry a granddaughter
of the headstones in the park cemetery,
I'm not part of this landscape.

As my boys fly down the slide at the park
by the train tracks and toss handfuls of pebbles
into the air, I find seeds stuck to my jacket
from my walk through the native grass. I pluck them
from fleece, four nearly transparent kernels,
set them on my palm and wait for the wind
to pick up and take them away.

Poetry by Linda Maki
New Life

Norway, 1885

Oh Jacob, she murmured, *the shame,*
the shame, and she moved to hide herself
in the folds of his old woolen coat.

Shush, little one. It is love, only love,
and he drew her in like a shuddering child.

I will not be forgiven.

We will not tell them,
it is our secret.

Mor will know. I will change
soon. She will know.

No one will know. I vow
to you. Our secret will be safe.

Not know, but how? Secrets
are never safe here.

Then we will leave here.

Leave? Norge? To be where?
People would follow. Sisters,
brothers, cousins, all the curious
who travel. They will come.

We will go far away, where no
one can find us, ever.

Amerika? she breathed.
Amerika, he promised.

Poetry by Kathleen J. Pettit
Winter

It has been cold, bone-shaking cold
The kind of cold that shrivels the will
Touches the primal in us that calls to hibernation
And the snow, instead of blanketing our world
Purifying it
Adorning it
Is smothering it in frigidity
Even the trees cry out with the weight of it
Our longing for warmth is lost only in deep slumber
Burying all hope that spring will find us
While the winds blow white

Fiction by Annie Stopyro
Sauna at Two Below

It's 240," he said, bursting in from the cold. "I propped the door open."

She pulled on a fuzzy robe and Crocs for the ten-foot journey, and when she stepped outside, the brightness of the midday sun on the snow was nearly blinding. She refused to close her eyes to the rare dose of vitamin D but couldn't look up exactly. It was 200 by the time she settled onto the smooth cedar slats, towel beneath her to absorb future sweat.

When he joined her, he carried a glass of beer. In his other hand was the bottle holding the remainder, which he snugged into the snow just outside the door. They had agreed to make it a work day, he on his paintings and she on her self-paced neurofeedback coursework. What place did beer have before this was fulfilled?

"Coffee bender," he said, as if in answer. "Up and down in one glass."

Her earlobes began to burn, and she eyed the thermometer. Her nipples grew erect, chafing with discomfort. Cupping them brought relief.

"I can help with that," he said.

She slid open the upper vent, breaking the seal of the heat. Soon she felt the first sweat droplet slide down her torso, from underarm to waist. A winter pleasure in a season she held for purpose, to delve into long, absorbing projects, without the distraction of the lake, its bays to be explored in slender gliding kayaks. Or the woods, where they went always on impulse, to sleep in a tent without a fly. These months, the only thing tugging at her was the warmth of the fire in the front room, where she'd already completed 57 hours. Certificate in hand before the snow melts, the goal.

"The feeder," he said, peering out through the vent, where a mob of fat birds with speckled bellies pecked and poked their long beaks at the nuts and seeds that mostly drew chickadees, cardinals, and juncos. She let her mind savor this new sound, the squeaky squabbles, though she knew starlings were unwelcome invaders in some minds.

"Ready for water?" he asked. After he dumped a ladleful over the rocks, she waited for it, the slug of heat that would belt her then dissipate steadily. It left her covered in a shiny mix of sweat and vapor. As he fed the furnace, she found herself sitting up taller as the muscles of her upper back began to grow longer and looser. She followed his gaze to the vent again, and they watched the steam gush out in powerful pillows, wafting past the starlings, who seemed unaffected by it. Did it feel warm to them? Or did it leave them soaked? Would ice crystals form as they flew away?

Zero. That's how many paintings he had done out of the sixteen that were expected right about the time the temperatures would rise to tolerable and they'd trade thick boots for rubber ones to navigate dirty puddles. It would happen like this. There would be no steady application day after day until completion, no calm climb, just a flattish line followed by a steep spike. In some frenzied charge of flying paint, there would be dabbed chaos and stroked despair. Self-absorption would flip-flop with deprivation, and suddenly something would appear on the canvas that he would call finished. Only caved-in wreckage would remain where once there was routine and peace, but he'd be finished. He would likely miss the deadline, but just by a hair, and it would be of no consequence.

When she was thoroughly drenched, she stood and wrapped herself in the towel knowing he would linger, until the hiss of water hitting rock was nothing more than a quiet *shhh*. On her way to the house, the warmth in her body overpowered what she knew was there but couldn't perceive, bracing bitter cold. From the kitchen window, she watched him emerge, barefoot, naked, striding across the ice-crusted wooden deck, white clouds heaving off his back in great swirls.

Poetry by Lina Belar
How A Century Farm Begins

Inside a small farmhouse where
women grind grain for the bread
while the wind blows, and the men
grunt and groan with the effort of
wresting a living from rock-laden soil,
through hot summers and bitter cold winters,
the grain, seed for next year's planting,
lies protected from heat and cold and wet
in a tightly sealed room with no windows
in the middle of the house.

Children are forbidden to play here.
Mice and rodents dare not chance the wrath
of the farmer's wife with her sharp blade.
Like fairy tale princesses, the seeds slumber
in safety, dreaming of languid summer days,
blue skies and occasional rain.

In spring, the door to the room is opened,
all but a small amount of the seed removed.
Fields are sown, produce grain for livestock.
Cows give birth, provide milk for their young
with enough left over for the human babies
who will soon grow large enough
to plant the seed, cut the grain, thrash it
and store it for the next generation
in the room with no windows
in the middle of the house.

Poetry by James L. Bettendorf
Late Summer in Minnesota

Give me one more September.
Let me be a child on a bed
of reds and browns and float.
Let me lie back in earthy piles
of brittle yellows and rumble
through a dry heap, inhale again
the dusky aroma. Let me roll,
leaf dust under my collar and in my
pants. Let me crush handfuls
against my face, taste the heady
scent of autumn and spit fragments
of fall from my mouth.

Fiction by Jerry Mevissen
Love. Birth. Death.

Whoever thought a moment so beautiful could last forever?

The bride and groom picked their way down the porch steps, over the slate rock path toward the pickup truck, its antenna decorated with a crude bow of red and white crepe paper. She bunched her long dress in one hand, clutched her bouquet in the other. The groom, thick wrists protruding beyond his sleeves, held her arm as she negotiated the uneven rock to the gravel drive. He opened the truck door and lifted her into the seat, then walked in front of the cab to the driver's side.

Two young boys, her brothers, ran behind the truck with a wire of tin cans and looped it over the rear bumper. The engine whirred, then roared, and the truck rolled forward. The mother wiped her eyes with an apron. The father steadied himself against a porch post, then hugged his wife, pulled her close, and waved. Ribbons on gifts fluttered over the tailgate as the truck rolled away. The boys chased the truck down the driveway laughing, the dog barking, the cans rattling.

At the road, the truck turned and the bride looked back at her family, now all waving, waving, waving. She rolled the window down and managed a half-wave, then disappeared behind a grove of Chinese elm that grew along the ditch.

Whoever thought a moment so beautiful could delay itself so long?

In those days, expectant fathers waited in the delivery room lounge, paging through old *Newsweek* magazines, feigning calmness, jolting when the doors swung open and Nurse McKay called *Mr. So-and-so, you have a baby boy.* And Mr. So-and-so, already a father, nodded his head, reached for his hat, and walked out. The rest sat, inhaling sterile hospital air, hearing an occasional muffled scream. Minutes passed, or was it hours? Days? The round clock above the swinging doors showed four, five, six o'clock. A.M. or P.M.?

Why don't you go to the cafeteria? Nurse McKay said. *It will be a while.*

Down the hall, down the stairs, past the cafeteria to the front door, he stood on the hospital entry and inhaled, exhaled, inhaled, exhaled. A light snow fell. Headlights and taillights indicated rush hour traffic. Morning or night? Why is her labor protracted? Will she be all right? Will the baby survive?

Back in the waiting room, Nurse McKay said, *You may come in for a few minutes.*

She lay on her back, knees bent, and forced a smile. Her skin was damp, her hair wet. He dabbed her with a towel, her forehead, her cheeks, her neck, her chest. She squeezed his hand with unexpected force, then placed it on her distended belly. *Soon,* she mouthed. *Soon.* Nurse McKay motioned for him to leave.

A muffled scream, another, another. He squeezed his eyes shut, gripped the arm rests, felt bile rise in his throat. Minutes passed. Quiet. The expectant fathers eyed each other. Yours? Mine? The red second hand on the wall clock swept around and around and around.

Nurse McKay opened the door, walked to him, and smiled. *You have a baby boy.*

He reached for her, attempted to stand, wobbled. Tears flooded his eyes, streamed down his cheeks. Tried to say *thank you* or something, anything. Nothing. *You can see her in her room in a few minutes*, she said.

He walked down the hall, down the stairs, to the chapel. He knelt, buried his head in his hands, and trembled.

He rose and walked to the hospital entry. Snowflakes swirled and levitated. He floated to the sidewalk and hovered over pure, fresh snow. He glided forward. Somewhere a carillon bell rang. He looked down at his side, extended a gloveless finger, and felt his son's tiny grip, saw his eager smile.

Whoever thought a moment of sorrow could be a moment of joy?

After her funeral, he led the procession with a team of

mottled Percherons that bore her coffin on a caisson down Main Street from First Lutheran to the graveyard. The church bell tolled, tolled, tolled seventy-nine times, one for each year of her life. When the *dust thou art* was dusted, the compulsory well wishes wished, the customary sandwiches consumed, he returned to the home place where they farmed and aged together. The kitchen was chilled and vacant, the bed lonely and depressing.

He moved to a small stuccoed bungalow with blue shutters on Main Street and built a garden in the front yard—annual flowers and perennial flowers that reminded him of her. The following year, he extended the garden to the side yard with roses and clematis, to the other side with tulips and daffodils, day lilies, and forsythia. The backyard remained intact, shaded by an orchard of apples and plums.

He attended the flowers with the love he attended her—careful soil preparation, timely food and water, constant cultivation. The garden responded, and flowers bloomed in primary colors and pastels—zinnias pink to red, marigolds yellow to orange, delphinium white to blue; in a variety of heights—crawling ground phlox to six-foot hollyhocks; in a jungle of shapes—spires of violet larkspur to mounds of copper asters.

Garden clubs drove from neighboring towns. The school art class sketched and painted the blooms. A reporter from the County newspaper photographed him in the garden and ran a story.

Flowers proliferated.

He carried bouquets to the church on Sunday, the Nursing Home daily, the Senior Center on lunch days. The clinic waiting room, the post office lobby, the tellers at the bank, the teachers at school, all received bouquets. Townspeople notified him of baptisms, birthdays, and anniversaries. They received bouquets. He delivered armloads of flowers, rose phlox bouncing off his shoulders, white daisies tickling his chin.

The summer passed, the garden flourished. His clientele grew and, in early September, when roses peaked and chrysanthemum burst into bloom and golden marigolds challenged the sun, he died.

The funeral service was brief, the attendance sparse. After the pallbearers lifted the casket onto the caisson, the church bell tolled, tolled, tolled. The team of Percherons clomped down Main Street leading the cortege toward the graveyard.

It passed the Senior Center, and diners, waiting and holding flowers, joined the procession. Passed the school where students stood in the parking lot, each with flowers. Passed Erickson Grocery where clerks flipped the OPEN sign, each holding flowers, and joined the procession. Passed the Nursing Home where residents waited in wheelchairs and on walkers, their caretakers steadying them, all carrying flowers. The bank, the post office, the feed mill, the hardware store, the clinic. Down Main Street, an undulating ribbon of colors—red and white and yellow and crimson and orange and violet, blue and pink and green and rose and coral and lavender . . .

Volume 24

Poetry by Steven R. Vogel
Winter Barn

I have a barn on the river
full stored with oats
and some corn.

The animals move about surely.
They have seen where I keep
the hay and are not concerned.

I wonder at them in their steam.
We have met many times—
they are not careful of me.

But how can they know my
intentions?
They do know, but postpone

their afflictions, I think.
They know winter will run out—
meanwhile, I will find them

huddled where I left them.
We have stumbled in the same
dropped ruts, have scathed

the same dark wind.
Their shallow curses are mine
for a long moment.

I grow weary of naming them
for their mothers,
but lineage surrounds them

to a fault. I know the stores
will run with the land,
and the land will run with me.

Poetry by Andrea Westby
Minnesota City in January

The city bathed in gold,
luminous grapefruit and tangerine light,
which makes it seem to contain warmth
it does not have

If you look closely,
even breath becomes a glittering cloud of white
all is edged with an icy blue and gray
eyelashes frosty white

No living being should be moving in air this cold

But the roadways are filled with ant-cars and tiny blinking lights
Stubbornness runs deep here

Defiant of nature's signs to
stop,
rest,
hibernate,
slow down

No, they say,
there is too much to do

Poetry by William Upjohn
Song for the Day

A bandit-masked woodpecker with a sun-
flashed crimson cap, enticed by the yard's trove

of treats flits from feeder to suet
to tree. Small flocks of finches

and sparrows arrive, feed,
fly away. A sudden turbulence

through the branches and shadows of oak
and ash as a sparrow darts, chased

by a Sharp-shinned Hawk that now banks,
levels off, now spreads its wings and rises

to brake, now glides in to perch
close to the tightly boughed pine in which

the sparrow sits.
The hawk waits.

I awake
from a caustic dream in which I'd escaped

calamity to the day pouring into my room;
wake to safety and the knowing

there is no need for flight
from this nest where I lie;

awake, with this sunlight,
now spilling

like birdsong,
across my bed.

Poetry by Margaret M. Marty
When the Blue Gentian Blooms

Working in the yard today,
my eyes tried hard to ignore
the weeds that bloom
along the perimeter in autumn.

But a rider inside my head
kept reining my neck to the left.
"Look, look," I heard him say,
"Drink in the beauty."

He was always one with nature—
loved the singing of the frogs,
the howl of the coyotes,
the honking of the geese.

Heralding the change of seasons
when fall harvest began,
his first words at suppertime,
"Babe, the blue gentian is blooming;
another year is going to bed."

How many more years must go to bed
until I awaken with you,
where the blue gentian forever blooms?

Creative Nonfiction by Steven R. Vogel
Trails

The first time he shot the cat with hot milk on a straight line from his one-legged stool, I thought only this: *I want to do that.* The cat was but one of any number of generic animals that held the warmer parts of the yard—that lived lives disdainful of us and our industries, our manners and cults. This one was patched and ragged, and skittish in the normal way of his fellows—he being a member of a loose congregation that could not be numbered, for all their comings and goings. His colors were irrelevant and impossible because the single bulb that strained far overhead shed only a scatter of light—light with dull edges and vast imperfections—into the thick dark of evening chores. We could see each other best out the sides of our eyes, each of us an approximate human apparition. The dark held back the scene so well it felt like strobe-lit space—like the bit of insight or knowledge that falls between flicks. But this feeling kept in a constant way inside that blousy barn. And now there were white, steaming lasers to split our attentions.

The passing years have dabbled the details, culling many of them, no doubt. But those that remain are more certain than yesterday's. I watched the cat whisk the dribs from his face with his paws and then follow up with a creature-like tongue that was apparently insensible to the dung dust that coated everything, even the air.

Who is he? What's his name? The cat had no name—no cat had a name, though every cow did. *He is here for the mice.* It was left for us to determine how the cats and the mice must have worked this undefined relationship.

But where does he live, and who cares for him? We knew that mice and rats, cousins in some way, lived behind the planked door of the oat bin, and we had peeked after them in husky daylight when it squeezed through the single pane high above it We dared go no farther than two steps into the banked oat slide not so much for fear of the rodents as for fear of the liquid aggression of the ramped feed: *Pull one scoop loose, and four will hurry after it—down and around and over, if you're not careful.* So, careful was a peek—a kick into the loose chaff near the door. Here must be a cat, for here must be a mouse. But

69

nothing moved beyond the oats.

Ten years later I would learn—on the bones of my back—the better home of mice, but that night we sat on anything that was not wet. We heard the wet breath of the cow surround the dry grind of oats and imagined how the machine of her must tamper with the grain to send it out as fluid nourishment. We listened to our grandfather's wet songs as they flowed to her back-turned ears. And I thought that I might hear the rasp of the cat's tongue as he scraped away proceeds. The mice were below us, listening for that very sound. We had always loved the springy, airy feel of the barn floor, the way it sloped up from the doors, the way we had to duck beneath stern rafters to get about the pens; but we did not know that trampled organic floor was cut through by a civilization of bucktooth scavengers who cared so much about the cat. They were most often as busy as they were quiet: busy hauling and strewing trails, busy cutting rooms like holes in cheese, busy counting down moments for runs to the oat bin.

They studied below us. They knew the small metallic sounds of white rain in a pail, the intervals of the squalls that went from teat to teat. They knew the clink of the handle, the strain of the pour, the cuss and smack that went from beast to beast. They knew the instant window, the time for a rush, where spilt foam might be found (adhered to several kinds of damp), the four routes for retreat. The cat knew all this and more.

But I thought only this: *I want to do that.* And so I wobbled on the two-by-four T, ignored the clanking hobbles, blinked against a purposeful tail, and pulled and pulled the unlikely pink leathers: warm, and wet and dry. There was only a small parenthesis of time before one of the participants would make the difference. The cat knew better than to wait. The rain, when it came, was slight and afraid—afraid of the scoured steel bucket that swept from my knees, that bounced to the wafered floor, that kicked past my senses, that spread its humble moisture to drip through the trails, into rooms, and down and around and over the least suspecting of us all. You will ask me how any of this could be so. I tell you that every word of it is true.

Poetry by Joseph E. Tietge
Feeding Chickens

The moon is as bright as I have ever seen it.

The reflected sunlight throws edgy shadows onto the snow
In monochromatic hues of lunar dust.
Then I see it in the sketchy resolve of peripheral vision . . .
My father's shadow,
as I go to feed the chickens.

Poetry by Laura L. Hansen
At Walden Pond in Business Suit and Heels

I should have known then
that I was on a wrong path,
should have turned away
from the office cubicles

and meetings, sometimes
three a day. I should have
spared myself the clenched-
jaw strain of the following

five years.
Outside of Boston
on the road to Concord
I already knew my own heart,

knew when I saw the small
arrowed sign for Walden Pond
and gasped and spluttered to
pull over/stop

that I was meant for water,
for small rough-hewn spaces
and silence. The writer in me
couldn't pass that tiny Mecca

without stopping to pay homage,
high heels sinking into the leaf
litter and loam, I knew home
when I saw it.

Poetry by Cheryl Weibye Wilke
Morning Campfire on Cloudy Day

I could almost hear them grumble
in unison, *City girl.*
The four fishing boats lined up near shore

on Lake Superior like beads on a string stretched
in a half moon. Grey-grizzled men watching
me attempt to start a campfire inside

the stacked-stone ring with a beer bottle
carton, bottom of a shoebox, two small
pieces of damp firewood and a half-
filled red, white and blue Diamond

pack of kitchen matches. There they floated
these early a.m. fishermen half-circling the stage
of the star of the show—silly old bear

of a woman. With back arched over
and knees folded nearly in prayer, I scanned
the bedrock for slips of bark, small

twigs, and pine needles to squeeze beneath
the disjointed heap. First, the smoke swirled
like notes from a flute. Then it burst

into flame. I thanked a Kokopelli-shaped piece
of dancing bark and the god of fire. Then I turned
toward the lake to take our bow.

Poetry by Rhoda Jackson
Under the Prairie Sky

Pastel beauty of Autumn beckons early this morning, a good day to
      clean bird
houses. One deemed unworthy by potential renters—"poor location and
      the roof leaks." I smile at
tiny blue feathers left behind on a pillow of twigs and straw. But then

I happen upon four emaciated Angels, fledglings entombed in a nest of
      Belonging.
What happened here? A Song sacrificed to provide Hawk's dinner?
      Or did Mother leave by choice?

Ancient Celts say the land remembers.
Memories of stone push to the surface beg to be heard,
create a cairn to honor what has been and what will be.

I continue my walk, cup of cooling sadness in hand,
pause to allow the breeze to catch up with my feet while I
search for the path of Serenity intersecting tragedy and joy.

Creative Nonfiction by Patricia Nelsen
The Ultimate Sanctuary

Riley! Riley, come here!" I beckoned to the orange tabby cat whose suspicious eyes peeked out from under the living room drape where he was watching the red light on the television power switch.

I pulled the box from the plastic Walmart bag. "Just for Cats," it announced. "Hide 'n Play." The multi-lingual container described it as "the ultimate sanctuary for your cat—*le refuge ideal pour votre chat!*"

The cat toy—*jouet pour chat*—was a plastic bag in blaze orange with bobcat-sized paw prints and the creator's name, Hartz, stamped in black on the top. Lime green and white tubing propped the entrance, on which were suspended multi-colored balls of yarn. It seemed a waste of color for an animal that only sees in black and white.

The refuge crinkled and rustled when Riley stepped inside. His eyes dilated to coal black, his paw swatted at one of the yarn balls, and thus he relinquished the drape hem and adopted the Hide 'n Play as his ultimate sanctuary.

How content Riley looked as he cuddled into a circular mound of fur, nose to tail, inside his refuge from the demands and cares of his cat world. I was consumed with envy. Little havens of tranquility are good for people, too.

My mind began collecting memories of former peace havens, away from the demands and cares of the people world. They were places of solace, rest and restoration—the relaxation of a bubble-resplendent hot tub, the over-stuffed chair with a fleecy blanket and a great novel.

After leaving McDonald's drive-through lane with a hot mocha latte lathered with whipped cream and topped with a cherry, I discovered my ultimate sanctuary. I was looking for a place to park so I could safely enjoy my caffeine concoction. The road led me to Sunnybrook Park on the edge of town. I followed the twisting tar roadway under the oaks and evergreens and pulled off on a small gravel spot between two towering white pines. The view overlooked a small rustic bridge, spanning a stream filled with gliding, honking Canadian geese. Squirrels darted nervously to the oak trees, their bristly, bushy tails flicking behind them. Startled blue jays registered disapproval with loud, raucous cries. A weeping willow tree clung to the creek bank and swayed in rhythm with the gentle breeze.

Reaching to the side of the driver's seat, I located the lever that converted it to lounge chair mode and took a sip of my mocha beverage, indulging in the splendor of nature amidst park placidity. On a hillside across the creek, the outline of a building was barely visible, shrouded in foliage of the trees that hugged it like a protective quilt. Lights blinked like fireflies between the leaves. I soon realized the lights were from the new dining room addition at Shady Lane Rest Home, where my mother had spent the last few years of her life.

As I blinked back a tear, memories of those years came flowing back. How long I had delayed the inevitable move from my home to the nursing home as physical failures took their toll on her frail body. The process began with repetitions of questions and statements, and then progressed to confusion about what things were called and who people were. The past became cloudy, hazy, and then totally dark. Present moments were like embers glowing dimly in the night. Forgetting the vital things—how to walk, how to eat—her eyes closed to the world outside of her own mind. It was time.

I wheeled her to the dining room that I now saw in the distance and fed her supper every evening. I sat at the foot of her bed and watched *Wheel of Fortune* as she napped. I took her for wheelchair walks on sunny days. I cherished my time with her, just being in her presence. When it was time for her to go, I knew she could not stay.

My search for an ultimate sanctuary led me to a place where I could share space with her once again. It seemed to have been guided by that mysterious coincidence that so often supplies us with exactly what we need.

I have been guided to a place where the voice in my head

says things like:
> "A stitch in time saves nine."
> "Many hands make light work."
> "Happiness is a state of mind."

The voice she lost is here in my ultimate sanctuary where I can connect past precious memories with present purposeful moments. In my ultimate sanctuary I can hear my mother's voice, full of wisdom and tenderness and understanding. I can listen while I sip my mocha latte and whisper, "I love you, Mom."

* * *

Poetry by Michael McCormick
Willow

He turns his gaze on me
Craggy eyes deep as wishing wells
Recognition
Dawning on his shaggy face

His mouth opens
He shouts
Green words that sound
Like wind and geese

Poetry by Meridel Kahl
Winter Ceremony

At true solar noon
when sun
at its
highest point
is low
one eagle
three crows
their shadows tall
on the snow
gather
on a shoulder
of highway
pick clean
the rib cage of a deer.

At dusk
when sky
shivers gold
at the end of a
tunneled forest
black wings clamor
to the tops of pines
white tail feathers
glide through
bare-fingered
branches of birch.

At midnight
Orion wraps stars
around white-bisque bones
left at the side
of a road.

I light
one candle
in a house
across the field.

Poetry by Charmaine Pappas Donovan
Heading into the Fog

Can this be what it will be like? I ask
hugging Dad through thick fabric,
layers warming his thin cool skin.
He is tired, no longer wants to argue.

He perches on life's slender edge,
his efforts to keep from falling a full-time job.
While others go about their daily routine,
he tends to his pills, his urinary needs,
chewing and eating, ten hours of sleep.

Though he is social,
there is little room for small talk,
friendships beyond family.
His world is shrink-wrapped
around his home's familiar clutter,
doctor visits, fluid intake and output,
TV's daily news and *Judge Judy.*

He says *I am ready to die,*
yet his thoughts are vague:
symptoms without a diagnosis.
He senses an unforeseen curve,
or his car stalled
on a drive into dense fog.
How? He gave up his car keys months ago.

This might be what it will be like, I answer
hugging his bony body good-bye,
bulky layers protecting his withered skin.
He is only twenty-one years older than I.

Poetry by Thomas C. Stetzler
Found
For My Grandfather

Late one afternoon
I ran away and got lost in the woods.

Toward evening, unsettling sounds
rose all around me,
voices sprouting up in the darkening hour.

Through the din, one small voice
came from afar
muffled by the deep woods.
I followed and the voice grew clearer.

At last
there you stood at the edge of the field,
lantern in hand
brimming with light.

Like a beacon, you were,
swinging that lantern,
calling me home
before all the trails
had grown over with night.

Creative Nonfiction Honorable Mention
by Audrey Kletscher Helbling
The Final Amen

Scent of lemon lingers. The rented shampooer, which moments earlier roared swaths across the living room carpet, idles in a corner. Windows sparkle. Paint dries in the guest bedroom.

My middle brother and I backward crawl across the dining room floor scrubbing scuffed linoleum, then curve around the kitchen peninsula.

We—five of six siblings, two sisters-in-law and my husband—have cleaned all morning at a steady pace. Laughing. Sometimes cursing. Often silent. Some drinking wine. I don't. It's too early for wine.

Rooms echo with emptiness.

The noon whistle blares. We gather in the kitchen, meatloaf steaming from the oven, paper plates stacked on the counter. Our heads bow. *Oh, give thanks unto the Lord . . .*

At the final amen, my grief quavers into words. "This is the last time we'll pray in this house. It's kind of sad." My middle brother, the property caretaker, glares at me. I don't care. Perhaps it's because I am the eldest daughter—the writer, the observant and introspective one—that I feel such depth of sadness. This 1950s rambler holds memories of five generations. Not just stuff emptied from rooms before the house goes on the market.

I smell oven-warm oatmeal raisin cookies, sauerkraut fermenting in a Red Wing crock, eggs frying in home-rendered lard. I sipped Dad's rhubarb wine here, savored spicy garden salsa, tasted the nip of fresh ground horseradish.

Even now I hear the steady rhythm of Grandma's treadle sewing machine and cousins chanting "Starlight moonlight, hope to see the ghost tonight" under a prairie sky stitched with an infinity of stars. I hear the murmurs of my mother's friends bearing comfort and hotdishes at the death of my father a dozen years ago.

Memories.

I imagine Grandma in the back bedroom, mottled hands lifting quilt tops pieced from fabric scraps. Show and Tell in her eighties. Proud. Stubborn, too. All German. Shock of white hair. Simple sleeveless cotton dress. Nylons sagging at her thick ankles. Grandma who hooked a garden hose to the tailpipe of her aged Chevy to gas moles ravaging her garden.

Beef roast on a platter. Boiled potatoes in a pot. Rich brown gravy. The staple foods of my people, served here, in this kitchen. And now this, the last meal, eaten at the dining room table carried from the house and set on the oil-stained garage floor.

We pray. *Amen.* I struggle with my sense of loss—loss of grandparents and father and now our mother moving from this house. Sadness furrows deep into my soul. No one seems to care. Or perhaps they do, but plant their feelings inside. We are German. Lutherans.

I circle the kitchen counter, fill my plate, weave my way to the garage. We laugh and talk like this is just another family dinner.

After we've eaten, my brothers grab the kitchen table, then heave it into the back of our nephew's pick-up truck. Another generation in another house in another town will gather around this table.

Oh, give thanks unto the Lord . . .

Poetry by Kim A. Larson
Only Jif

*I*s *there any other?* he would say
and order dry, which meant no butter,
and dark, which meant burnt—toast.
None of this warm bread, he'd say
every morning at the restaurant
that didn't serve Jif. He brought
his own jar, the large economy size,
smooth not crunchy, spread on so thick
it wouldn't melt. Each slice cut into thirds.
He wasn't as fussy about his jelly, yet
he preferred strawberry to grape.
A teaspoon of jelly preceded each bite,
not smeared but mounded on top
in the shape of the spoon. In sync with
his mouth his eyes opened wide, a soul
patch of hair squishing into his beard.
Three bites per row, nine bites per slice,
seven days a week Jif peanut butter toast
with jelly. Over seventy-eight years of life,
more than half a million bites.

Poetry by David Eric Northington
London Fog

Smoke-filled room of failure
Like an imitation London Fog
Rock music on an eight track player
Songs repeating tracks one through four
Scribbled notebook paper on the front seat
The big V8 stumbles then quits running
Music slows then stops as gas runs out
Ticking from the hot engine block
The sounds no one can still hear
Finally the overhead door slides open
Exhaust smoke escapes betraying its guilt
Red lights hurried motions hours too late
Done just for the family's sake
35 years later remembering that night
An older brother died alone

Poetry Honorable Mention and Editor's Choice
by Susan Niemela Vollmer

Remains

He wanted his ashes spread here
in the river where he fished each day
among the swans and the eagles
with bass jumping and water rippling
deep within his bones

His partner had a different plan
instead he will lie with her
and her former husband
in a distant state he never planned to visit
an unquiet triad along the forested slopes

Whenever we pass this spot
where he planned to rest
we glimpse his shadowy silhouette
in his boat at sunrise
mist drifting like ashes above the water

Poetry by Justin Watkins
Deer Camp circa 1940
(after looking at a family photograph)

This is rough-sawn lumber
A slant ceiling and somber walls
What is needed is here

Wood fueling fire warming air
Fire heating iron boiling water
This all for the men

Each in coarse wool wear
Resting on bare mattresses
Rising to clasp a shoulder

Holding simple metal cups
For there is no gadgetry here
Only a membership

They who have stared steady
Down steel into the heart
The warm beating heart

They who have knelt in the cold
With hands on the light of the forest
And watched it color the snow

Poetry by Sandra Howlett
Bois Sauvages
Inspired by an oil painting of the same name by Mary Jo Van Dell

The darkness feels heavy
as if it could crush me with one swift brush
of its hand, pinning me down, pressing on my lungs
so that I have to think
about my breathing
or it will not come.

Sometimes I'm like the dark pines
piercing the light, tall and jagged like daggers—
I want to stay in the darkness, silent
suffocating
but somehow safe.

Other times my trembling branches,
tired of bracing the raging winds,
reach out to the light above the dank forest
looking for salvation, hope
a new perspective from above
like a god
or an eagle on the hunt.

Poetry by Ruth Jesness Tweed
The Man in Room 22

Unseeing eyes look across the room,
no reply to my greeting.
I wonder what might be behind the stare.
Does he remember his childhood?
His pranks?
His loves?
His life?
Does he nod in prayer learned at his mother's knee?

Or is this as it seems—the demon of dementia
that leaves an empty shell?
Does he remember the struggles?
Blizzards and dust storms?
Failed crops?
War?
Recall the sad goodbye as the troop train pulled away?
Can he see the fallen comrade on the jungle floor?
Does he grieve for children never born?
Does he suffer again his bride's last hour of pain?

Or is he now at peace
in the gentle fog
of forgetfulness?

Creative Nonfiction by Janet Thompson
The Puzzle

It was early November in North Dakota. Perry and I arrived to help bring his dad home from the hospital. Our hearts soon told us we could not leave Mom and Dad alone with the challenges of the new physical and emotional demands.

Several days into our stay, Perry and I ran a few errands. At one store I found a stack of puzzles. My eyes stopped on one box containing a cabin. Its windows, with their golden glow, reminded me of home. In the yard sat a beautiful classic pickup, much like the one Perry drove when we dated. We brought it home, thinking its 1000 pieces would help occupy our anxious hearts. It ended up showing us answers to questions we didn't know we had.

We started by separating the colors. The puzzle contained a beautiful blue classic truck. I said in high expectation, "Let's start with the truck!"

We struggled until our daughter Nicki came over, took one look, and said, "What's wrong with you two? Puzzles 101, do edges first!" With patient diligence, she put all of the edges together, achieving order and rhythm.

Like our puzzle start, so was our care-giving for Dad. Perry and I swooped in and immediately looked for the beautiful. We started in the middle, led by our hearts and emotions.

Dad had said to us, "Don't let those damn hospice nurses hover over me." When Dad spoke, you listened. So, warning them aside, we assumed the hovering role. I'm sure that was no less annoying to him, but when you love and care deeply, it's so damn hard not to hover.

When we stopped hovering, the nurses and Perry's cousin Tammy stepped in. They knew what was needed. With experience and skills, they moved forward. They took what was beautiful, in a difficult setting, and put order and rhythm to it.

We had wonderful visits from family and friends during this

time. Many stepped over to look at the puzzle. Most tilted their heads, many scratched their chins, some pulled up a chair to join in, others stepped back and said, ". . . it's too hard . . ."

The reactions to the puzzle were often reflected in the visits. Some popped in for a short visit as their handshake said, ". . . it's too hard . . ." Others sat down, adding words and stories that merged past with present. Neither is right or wrong, both respected and understood. Different times, different people, different ways.

Some laugh at puzzles. They threaten to sneak a piece away. They mix colors up. They look for the joy in fellowship.

We joined around Dad's bed with effusive stories of days gone by. We read cards of encouragement aloud and held the phone close to Dad's ear during calls. We tapped our toes, clapped, and laughed as Dad's grandsons, Andy and Jason, played their guitars. Happiness. Togetherness. Joy in what we have . . . even when the picture seems incomplete.

Our daughter-in-law Holly came quietly in, sat down at the puzzle and completed more in three hours than we did in three days. Another morning, Perry's Uncle Frank came and sat beside me. We spoke little; it wasn't necessary. Together we accomplished much.

Anonymous hands spent hours preparing meals, cleaning rooms, fixing pipes, hauling garbage: few words exchanged but much help given. Many do not desire rewards but will complete tasks that give freedom to others. They see what needs to be and they do.

One morning I sat at the puzzle and things just began to click. My brother-in-law Jeff sat down to bring a different perspective to the puzzle. Piece after piece fell into place. Six pieces and the blue sky would be complete. Wait—two pieces don't fit. But they had to . . . They had to go there . . . They were BLUE! There was absolutely no other place for them to go and . . . they didn't fit.

My heart sank. Did so many of us spend the last week, only to come to this point and find we had a defective puzzle? Who would be so cruel as to purposefully design a puzzle that didn't fit together?

Looking back, Dad's illness seemed like those two mismatched puzzle pieces. A strong, vibrant man, full of life suddenly tossed into a world of emergency rooms, surgeries, and chemo treatments. It doesn't fit.

How could we get the pieces to fit in this otherwise perfect puzzle? Finally, in acceptance, I took a dozen or so pieces apart to attempt a new finishing point. I steered toward a new resolution.

I think Dad worked with his cancer diagnosis this way. Not only did life for Mom and Dad suddenly meet a radical change, but so it did for family and friends. Day to day expectations and priorities get buried in a rock slide leaving us to navigate with new maps.

It almost seemed like Dad was waiting for us to finish the puzzle . . . "Can't leave a job half done." Nine days had passed and there were things back home that needed attention. Perry would stay while I went home. As I sat in the wee hours of that morning, torn and in tears, Dad's words echoed through my head, "Stop that damn hovering!" As much as it broke my heart to leave, I knew that's exactly what Dad would want me to do. There's other life to attend to; it was not my job to finish the puzzle.

Two days after I returned home, Perry sent a text about the puzzle. It simply read "Done!"

The next day the telephone rang. "Dad's gone."

Embrace the pieces with others: a completed puzzle is a work of beauty . . . and love.

Poetry by Arnie Johanson
Home Hospice Care

The meals these days are maybe half
as good as when she cooked. A lot of bread,
simple salads, mac and cheese, mountains
of Stouffer's lasagna.

        Cuisine's not all
that's declining in this place. Detritus gathers
in every kitchen corner on floors that were immaculate
before the cancer moved into her brain, her bones
and half her other organs.

        There's nothing now
can bring her back to what she was, but she's still
my wife, teaching her one good hand to use
a spoon and fork, fighting to maintain self-control,
go places unaided. Nook on knee, she looks at me.
Her eyes beg forgiveness
        for what she's doing to me.

Poetry by Peter William Stein
Miscarried

I was careless, the egg
dropped to the kitchen floor.
The yellow

resembled a sun hanging
on the horizon. The egg white ink blot
a negative space displaying

what could have been—
egg in a blanket, a Denver omelet,
a deviled egg.

I never considered
her hunger as she waited
at the table, sick

to her stomach,
phantom pains of little
kicks to her ribs.

Not crying over
spilled yolk, I wiped the floor
and fixed breakfast.

Poetry by Scott Stewart
one shoe

there's one shoe under the foot of the bed
there's one shoe out in the car
there's one shoe on the side of the street
one shoe left at the bar
there's one shoe halfway up on the stairs
or is it halfway down
one shoe by the rides of the fair
one's on the school playground

there's one shoe by the lake near a cabin
one on the edge of town
. . . with so many half-shod people out there
how do they all get around

Creative Nonfiction by René Bartlett Montgomery
My Nothing Special Afghan

The white afghan drapes over the old wooden rocking chair that sits on the blue rug in my living room. The rug came from an inexpensive three-piece set quickly purchased at Menards when we first moved into this house. The rocking chair came as a package deal with a few eclectic furniture pieces the former home owner left behind. My mother did not spend late nights rocking me to sleep in this chair, nor did my grandmother sit in it as she crocheted in front of her wall-mounted electric fireplace in the family home on Linzie Road. I have no great stories to tell about them.

The afghan doesn't stand out much either. The simple pattern repeats, with bobbles running up and down in rows between crochet chains that crisscross the surface and end on two fringed sides. It looks a lot like every other afghan I have ever seen. I don't remember how I came to have this blanket. Grandma did not strive to finish it as a *Piece de resistance* just in time for my wedding day. I did not receive it in honor of a child's birth, or as a comfort for the loss of a dear one. No one spent hours in yarn shops painstakingly selecting skeins with just me in mind. In fact, the yarn came from a big box of craft supplies purchased at a garage sale. Yet I hold on to it as a treasured gift because Grandma will make no more. She will not pick out yarn and patterns. She has no more quiet time to sit and rock and craft. The house on Linzie Road, with its little electric fireplace, sold long ago, and the home my family shared with her after that recently sold.

Family, friends, houses, cars, recipes have all moved on but I still have that afghan, and it has a little of Grandma's heart and soul stitched within it. On a cold winter night, that simple afghan has the power to embrace all of me, like Grandma did when I was small. I settle into the warmth as I sit, during my own quiet time, in front of my fireplace, rocking in my left-behind chair on the cheap blue rug, stitching my own heart and soul onto needles and into yarn.

Poetry by Annaliese Gehres
Metaphor

Is there a metaphor
that will not seem trite to you
that I can summon
to capture this feeling
of emptiness?

Is there a metaphor
I can use
when my daily life goes on
just the same
yet my world forever changed?

Is there a metaphor
great enough to hold her
my grandmother
one who did not cloak
herself in fairy tales
who did not try to be original
who was just herself?

Is there a metaphor
great enough
to shed light on my loss
a grief that is really
straightforward
and everyday?

Sometimes reality is not colorful
enough to make a great poem
that will wow its readers
leaving them pondering new ideas

Sometimes metaphors
seem like
sacrilege
and the most comfort
is in the timeworn
time-tested phrases
commonplace prayers
and ordinary tears.

Fiction Honorable Mention by Paula L. Hari
FAQs

These were the FAQs every time they ended up in the emergency room at Saint Joseph's.

Medications?

Allergies?

Prior surgeries or hospitalizations?

Collette had become smarter or at least more prepared in the years since her father had up and died and left her mother dying of a broken heart. She'd compressed the complex medical history that was her mother into a five-page document and kept a copy in her purse. Beverly had never been healthy. Her husband's unexpected death had exacerbated the situation.

Collette handed the summary to the nurse who began to read: current medications, allergies, medical diagnoses. The nurse's eyes widened when she got to the pages of surgeries and hospitalizations. She tucked the document under Beverly's most recent information. Then she asked her FAQs anyway.

"Current medications? Allergies to meds? Prior surgeries or hospitalizations?" Collette wanted to say, *It's right there.* Instead she sat and listened to her mother answer, always amazed that someone with only an eighth grade education could rattle off the names of two dozen medications, the recommended dosages and common side effects and the reasons she took them. Beverly knew more about her meds than a lot of ER staff they'd encountered.

"Ranexa? Can you spell it for me?"

"R-A-N-E-X-A. Ranexa."

"You're taking it for?"

"It's a long actin' nitroglycerin for angina. It ain't used very often but it works for me. Better than that nitro spray they used to give me. This stuff don't give you no headaches." Collette winced at the double negative. Her mother moaned.

Then came the ten thousand dollar FAQ.

"Are you in any pain right now? Rate your pain from one to ten with one being no pain at all and ten being unbearable."

Her mother moaned. "Ten." It was always a ten, punctuated by a moan or a sob. The nurse patted Beverly on the arm. "We'll get something as soon as the doctor gets in here." She turned to Collette and said, "Poor thing." Collette imagined she meant her and not her mother.

After the Percocet, Collette sat with the curtain drawn and listened to the slow hiss of the oxygen pumping in syncopation with her mother's shallow, labored breathing.

She should call her husband. Instead she played Words with Friends, drank her third Diet Coke, and did some Facebook stalking: Lydia's son made the "B" team in hockey. Marie was "feeling inspired" after her five mile run. Allison was looking forward to date night with her hubby. Collette thought of what her post would read: *Collette is feeling snarky. Another day wasted at the ER with Beverly.*

She dialed her husband at work and left the latest variation of her usual message. "At the hospital with Mom. Again. She called an ambulance. Again. They're running the usual tests. Call you later." He knew the drill too well.

As if on cue, Beverly moaned for her dead husband, calling out his name. Collette remembered how her dad used to feign sleep in his recliner until she changed the channel on the television. "I was watching that," he'd say, one eye opened, peering at her. She smiled until the doctor pulled the curtain and said, "Mrs. Langdon."

Beverly's eyes fluttered half-open. She was too far into the Percocet to answer any FAQs now. He shook her arm and spoke to the glassy eyes. "We didn't find any evidence of a stroke. Your blood work is within normal ranges. No sign of kidney or liver failure. Aside from your heart condition and your advanced stage of deteriorated health, there is nothing medically wrong."

He turned toward Collette. "You are the daughter? This is your mother?"

Collette didn't hear the question mark. *You are the daughter.*

This is your mother. Silently she screamed, *This is not my mother. This woman is nothing but a glob of sticky lungs and brittle bones, held together by a patchwork of surgeries. You're wasting your time. My mother has been gone for a long time.*

"Yes, she's my mother."

The doctor scribbled the discharge and said, "We really have no reason to admit her. A social worker will come and talk to you about her discharge." *More FAQs,* thought Collette.

Do you feel safe in your home?

Can you care for yourself?

Do you have a support network?

"Any other questions?" he asked.

She dismissed her own FAQs and willed him to ask the NAQ, the never asked question: *Do you want to continue living, Mrs. Langdon?*

But she answered instead, "No. Thank you, Doctor, for your time."

"At this rate, your mother doesn't have much of *that* left."

Collette said, "Tell her that. It's what she wants to hear."

Poetry by *Charmaine Pappas Donovan*
Nursing Home Routine

I notice he lists to one side in his geriatric chair
when I step into the doorway of Station 5's dining room.
As I approach, he searches with half-vision, for recognition.
I lean close, say, "Hi, Dad," then I fling my jacket over a chair.
I adjust his plaid clothing protector,
fill glasses with his favorite honey-thick liquids,
only slow-sliding drinks since his stroke.
His foothill cheekbones make the rest of his face chasm.
He is nose and eyes, and big ears, now that his hair is short.
Slowly he spoons baked beans into his mouth,
moves a few meat balls around the edge of his plate,
pushes the plate away.
                    I try to pull it back,
but he waves his good hand, says he has had enough.
He will drink his milk, his juice and, if I coax him,
gulp down a malt made from a Magic Cup and milk.
I wheel him to his room where we brush his teeth.
He shaves while I wash his spit into the toilet.
After I set out his clothes for the next day,
I lean him back in his chair, blanket him
and turn the channel to *Wheel of Fortune.*
I kiss his forehead and say, "I love you."
Usually he says, "I love you, too," but sometimes
I am beyond him, dismissed like one of his past pupils.

Poetry by Georgia A. Greeley
This Time

It's not my job; it's his.
But here I am
imagining little squares
and pushing the mower back and forth,
cutting all the living things
within each squared-off space.

It's not my job; it's his.
I choose to mow around the flowers,
around each beautiful pink and yellow columbine.
He wouldn't; but he's not here.
I am. So there.

It's not my job; it's his.
So there again.
As I mow each off-kilter square,
I push the "so there" in front of me,
make precise turns,
behead plants that bleed green.

But this time, it is my job; he's not here.
Even angry, eventually, I get lost in the motion.
Back and forth. Back and forth.
I start to imagine my own work springing
from this Zen-like, patchwork movement.

> > >

He's not here.
And I miss him most in the silence;
it isn't thick enough.
Our bed seems off balance, only one side filled.
So I take action. Move in little squares.
Back and forth. Back and forth.

He's not here.
For two to three months,
this job is mine.
He said he would return.
He said so.

Fiction Honorable Mention by Larry Ellingson
Another Man's Treasure

Guy looked across the table at his son and daughter. "What am I supposed to do with her collections?" he said. "The house is full of stuff. For years I kept asking her to get rid of it, sell it somewhere. It never got done . . . it just kept growing."

Katelyn slouched over the kitchen chair, thumbing her cell phone as she spoke. "There's no hurry with all of that, Dad. Just take some time to get adjusted." She straightened and looked up at Rob and her brother jumped in.

"That's right Dad. Just give it time. We'll give you a call next week to see how you're doing."

Guy's children had helped him to figure out the insurance and the joint accounts, his bills were caught up and the funeral expenses paid, closets and drawers were cleaned out. They were tired and wanted to get back to their own homes. They had jobs that were waiting, their kids had to get back to school; there were a million things.

The collecting started small and went from there. Guy slogged up the final hill of his career and was thinking about retirement. Rob and Katelyn finished college and got their first jobs. About that time, Laura began going to thrift shops and flea markets, sometimes taking two or three day trips to antique shows. Things began to appear. Sets of glassware, bright shining cups and saucers, dishes in green and red and blue. This was followed by an assortment of painted plates. Soon there was a display case devoted to colorful pots and then another to little porcelain figures, posing in Bavarian cuteness. At some point, one collection was packed away and a different set appeared, and then another and another, each collection boxed and put away as it was replaced. Before long the basement was full of boxes, neatly labeled and stored. For what? A bigger house? This accumulation of things had been so gradual that he hadn't noticed how it had grown.

He couldn't crack the code of things that she collected. It seemed purely random. The only consistency was that she wouldn't, or couldn't, stop at one object. He began to suspect that there was some underlying cause. Isn't there a fine line between collecting and hoarding? Maybe she was compensating for something? An empty nest syndrome? Some unconscious need to compensate for her impoverished childhood? Maybe she had tapped into the same primitive urge that causes some animals to gather shiny objects and squirrel them away. Guy preferred to avoid conflict, but he played out internal arguments with her. He imagined confrontations and demands leading to boxes of knickknacks going out the door to the second hand store.

Guy was a month into retirement when the bright novelty of having time on his hands began to tarnish. "Let's get away for a few days. We always talked about doing some camping and hiking when we had time," he suggested.

Laura looked up. "That was years ago. We were younger and could crawl into a tent and sleep on the ground . . . I cannot do that anymore," she said. Guy knew that the emphasis on "cannot" meant that no amount of persuasion would convince her that this was a good idea.

"Well, how about if we plan a winter trip, somewhere warm . . . desert hiking or a nice beach with palms?" said Guy, feeling vague and slightly irritated.

"I was afraid that this might happen," Laura said.

"What?" Guy asked.

"That you would get bored," she said. "You always need to be doing something. Why can't you just enjoy the moment? Go fishing or get a hobby, for heaven's sake!"

Guy thought that retirement might bring them closer, but instead it magnified their differences. Laura became more focused and passionate about the things she collected. She picked up books about the artistry and history behind this particular type of glass or this style of pottery. She would tell Guy about them but it only annoyed him.

When they were alone together, once comfortable silences became awkward moments. Eventually he stopped paying attention and she stopped sharing. Guy could feel the heat of their relationship dissipating, like the chilling of a warm current at the mouth of a river as it empties into a cold lake.

When Laura died, his grief collided with other feelings: freedom, renewal, a sense of purpose. He didn't know what the purpose was yet; it was still just a sense, but he thought that he would figure it out and that it would be interesting and exciting. He reasoned that if he unloaded some of the flotsam in his life, the detritus she had gathered, that it would help him to get his bearings.

There was a flea market every other Saturday. Guy knew that his wife often went to it, and it was there that he thought he could begin to get rid of some things. He left the house early, paid for a space and unpacked two boxes of glassware, intending to sell cheap. Other sellers arrived and began to set their things out on tables. Guy recognized one of the sellers from his wife's funeral; the memory fixed in his mind like an exposed image. The man had reached out and put his hand on the lid of her casket, gently resting it there. He stood quietly for several minutes and then left, not staying for the lunch. The man was trim and lean and gray-bearded and he smiled faintly as he crossed the lot toward Guy.

"Good morning. I'm John," he said, extending his hand.

They shook. "Mornin'. I'm Guy."

"Yes, I know. I knew your wife. She came here regularly and we became friends."

"Oh?"

"Everyone here knew her. She knew a lot about antiques . . . and she could drive one hell of a bargain."

"Didn't I see you at her funeral?"

"Yes, I was very fond of her." His eyes went to the glassware and picked up the shine. "She was bright and funny and I . . . we, all of us here, miss her very much."

"I miss her, too," Guy replied in his widower's tone. "But she brought a lot of stuff home from these sales, and now I need to get rid of it."

Their eyes locked for an instant and Guy suddenly felt vulnerable, that he had exposed a weakness.

"I'd be glad to take it off your hands," John said. "All of it, in fact."

"Really? You would buy it all, sight unseen?"

John laughed. "Well, I've probably seen most of it. We bought and sold to each other for several years. I have an antique store and I'm sure I can sell it. How about if I come by tomorrow, look everything over and see if we can agree on a price?"

Guy agreed, pleased with himself and thinking how Kat and Rob would be surprised at how quickly he was taking control of his life.

John dove into her collections as if it was a reunion with old friends. Every box contained a story: where this item was purchased, who saw it first, what was paid and why it was a good buy. After going through the boxes, he went through the display cases, smiling knowingly at some of her pieces. When he came to the porcelain figurines he noticed the figure of a girl and boy, alpine hikers striding in step, hand in hand. He picked it up and held it in both hands, studying their timeless child faces. He was quiet for a long minute. Finally he said, "We had a lot of fun together. She was always ready for an adventure, you know. She had this childlike wonder of the world, seeing shapes and colors and textures that I had long ago quit noticing. When we were together, she made me feel like I was a visitor to a foreign country, where everything is new and different." He carefully wrapped the figure in tissue and put it in his pocket. "I'll keep this one to remember her by."

After John packed up the boxes and left, Guy sat and looked around him. He thought about John and Laura. He tried to rouse his anger but it wouldn't take hold. It had been his doing. He had let something go, even before it was lost. He and Laura had had moments of quiet enjoyment, good times relived, but he had no recent memories of shared happiness. Now he wanted to feel that resonance again, the sympathetic vibration that lovers feel. He wanted to experience surprise and discovery with her. He longed to feel the contentment that came after making love, limbs entangled, floating in warmth and peace and fullness. A light rain spattered the window. The day's light was fading and the house felt damp and cold. His eyes wandered around the slowly darkening room and landed on the shelves and spaces where all the bright and colorful things had been.

Poetry by Jeanne A. Everhart
Waiting For All Saints Day

This cool October morning's breath
exhales silent apparitions ascending
from the smooth surface of the lake
wisp spirits on feather feet float
in the stillness toward the rising sun

a shroud veils the island where
a lone white birch tree stands
sentinel of this autumn daybreak
leafless gnarled fingers branch upward
trying to escape the ghostly fog

Fiction by Susan Koefod
In the Margins

The first time I heard her name I was a teenager, and I was told it would be the only time I'd hear it, so I wrote it down in my diary as soon as I could.

I had immediately demanded more details as I knew it would be my one chance. Mother wasn't much for small—or any other—talk.

"I thought you should know her name," she said.

She wouldn't even say the word *adopted*. She spoke a name and nothing else.

I begged for more.

"You don't want to know more," she said.

I threatened to run away.

Mother wasn't one to give a direct look either. But right then she did, looking me full in the face, her expression hostile. Was she evaluating whether I was ready to hear the truth? Or feeling threatened? Another mother might have grown teary when forced to admit that the child she had raised was another woman's. The longer she looked at me, the angrier she got. Didn't she know what was best for me? My questioning an affront to her parental judgment?

It was then I learned about the asylum. That I'd been taken from my birth mother just before she had been committed. Mother and Father received a knock at the door one winter night, and child-abandonment officials handed me to them. Mother and Father were childless and had contacted the county hoping for just such a situation. Papers were drawn up listing them as my parents and a guessed-at birth date from the summer before.

"You don't need to know more," Mother told me.

For years that was all I had: her name, fragments of my birth story, stern reminders from Mother that we would never speak of her again. I determined I'd have to go it alone, and began to formally search for her when I was living on my own, but was immediately denied access to my own birth record and any death records at the county courthouse. Without a date, without a birth certificate listing both of our names, or any other official record that connected us, I left empty handed. I even combed the census records from the time, but never recognized a name that could have been hers.

Even the asylum wasn't giving anything else up about her: it had long been shuttered, its tragic secrets locked behind a high fence and an electronic security system. I knew there was a cemetery on the grounds, but so many inmates had been buried in unmarked graves that even if I'd been allowed in I would have learned nothing. I searched through old phone books in the town library where the asylum was located, soon giving up as there were so many names and so many years had come and gone.

I found the adoption papers when I was boxing up Mother and Father's things after Mother died at eighty, ten years after Father had passed. My hands shook as I read and reread my birth mother's name, the date she formally gave me up, and my name. Finally I could narrow down my search, so I started over, searching the census records and phone books once again, but still not finding her. Had she never left the asylum? Never gone on with her life somewhere else?

I learned that with special clearance, I could look at the asylum director's journals, which were kept in a secure library at the county courthouse. The adoption papers were enough to grant me the clearance I needed. I paused then. For a year, then another, driving past the sturdy brick courthouse building more than once, stopping out front, and panicking at the thought of climbing the solid concrete stairs and going inside. Maybe Mother had been right, as stern as her judgment sounded so many years before.

I was afraid of learning too much, too little, or nothing at all. Each option seemed equally damning. I had stopped short of many other important decisions in my life. Men came and went. The chance to marry and raise my own family passed me by. I told myself that it was because I didn't know that I could take risks. Because maybe I was too much like my birth mother, and I couldn't be trusted to care.

By chance one day an errand in town left me with hours to

kill. Before I could think about it too much, I climbed the concrete stairs and made my way to the secure library. The archivist handed me a sheet of instructions, and made me sign a paper that informed me of my liability in handling the director's journals: I could be prosecuted if I caused any damage. She had me put on a pair of cotton gloves, intended to keep the oils and perspiration of my hands from harming the fragile materials. Then she wheeled a cart inside the locked archive room, put a flat box containing several years worth of journals on it, and left the cart and box next to me, telling me I'd have until the library closed to review them.

I read the director's notes from that day she was committed. I wasn't sure how long my courage would hold out—waves of nausea came and went, my hands trembled, and my breathing was shallow and fast. I rubbed my eyes and sat back in the chair, willing myself to slow down. I'd made it inside and didn't necessarily need to hurry through, but I couldn't completely squelch my fear that I'd learn too much or too little. So be it, I told myself. If I had to, I would define her by all the empty space around her as if I were snipping a sheet of black paper to create a silhouette. In which case, I'd need to pay even more attention to what I could learn. I took several deep breaths, and went on.

The director carefully recorded that the temperature was below zero, the snow was up to the first floor windowsills, and one unfortunate patient was found frozen to death on the grounds. While the height of the snow made for an attractively higher landing spot for that inmate's escape plan, the frigid temperatures put an end to it. The director wrote the weather report and its impact on the escapee on the bottom of the page, under the heading "Discharged/Deceased."

She was the only patient, or more accurately, inmate, admitted to The Asylum for the Dangerously Insane on that day. Under "Admissions" he had written my mother's name only. In the margin, the director had dashed off "She was tiny and thin, with yolk-colored hair and albumen skin."

"Albumen skin" seemed insulting, as if he were describing a broken egg and not a person. The phrase sounded like the words from an autopsy: his prognosis that she was destined never to leave the place alive.

Still, the director had been struck enough by her to make a hurried note in the margin. Nowhere else in the journal had I seen anything like what he wrote: all the rest of the writing was kept within the margins and there were no other physical descriptions of any other arriving inmates.

I spent a few more hours combing through his other journals up until the date corresponding with census records I'd already researched from the era. Forty pages of men and women who were at the asylum the date of the census and not a trace of her. I'd hoped that meant she had left town after being released from the asylum, and went onto a fulfilling life elsewhere. But there was no record of her in the "Discharged/Deceased" section of his log either. She had been admitted, then disappeared, whited out the moment she stepped within.

I glanced at the clock and saw that my time was nearly up, several hours quickly elapsing as I paged through the journals. There was nothing more to learn about her except that she was tiny and thin, with yolk-colored hair and albumen skin.

She would never be more than an absence from my life. She would always be defined by the negative space that enveloped her. I quietly slipped off one of the gloves, kissed my finger, and ran it across the words, leaving a trace of myself on the one portrait I had of her: an asylum director's notation in the margins.

Poetry by Meridel Kahl
Kumihimo
the Japanese textile art of braiding

I.

A thousand years ago
Buddhist monks
plaited satin threads
into cords of color
to quiet
their minds.

II.

Six hundred years ago
Samurai clansmen
fastened bits of
lacquered armor
with twined ribbon
to shield
their hearts
and lungs.

III.

Tomorrow
I will sit
with friends
in a cafe
drink cups of tea
gather strands
of our words
into swirls of
magenta and indigo
and gold
weave them
into braids
necessary
as breath.

Poetry by Laura L. Hansen
Saving the Trees

We should write our poems upon the birch
still standing in the forest, in the sand
along the beach.

We should inscribe our words on the wet rock
of the shore, on the rising banks
of snow.

We should take as our pen the icicle
that hangs near the door, the willow branch
stripped by the wind.

Let the trees stand. We'll not need them
for paper anymore,

for our words shall be carried off by birds
like last year's seeds, berry red and bold.

Fiction by Cheyenne Marco
Still Waters

The tingling in Olivia's fingertips crept through her knuckles to her right wrist and up to her elbow. She clenched her hand into a fist and ignored it as she had all summer. It started right around the time they'd started talking about shutting down the gas station. She chalked it up to stress, and nothing relaxed her more than the lake. She approached the water's edge and let her thoughts ebb and flow with the waves. The moon bleached everything into shadows. The mosquitoes buzzed in harmony, not exactly breaking the silence—somehow using their song to bring her to the silence behind it. She took a deep breath of fish and orchid; at once, the combination was a perfume and a poison.

They said she just came home from college one summer and stayed. Then again, that's how it was with everyone in Stillwater. They were the ones that stayed. Despite the lack of jobs, the freezing winters, the closed school, and the whopping 364 residents, someone always found a reason to return. For most, it was family or financial. For some, it was love or loss. For others, it was just home.

For Olivia, it was the lake.

In the Land of 10,000 Lakes, this one was easily overlooked. It was no more than a mile wide and—at most—six feet deep. The beach held more rocks than sand. However, its most defining flaw flourished in the heat. On days over eighty, algae blooms flowered, and the water turned greener than a suburban lawn. When Olivia was a child, her father explained to her how the spring rains washed fertilizer into the lake and that the lack of outflow trapped the nutrients. The still waters that inspired the name of the lake created the perfect home for algae.

While others pinched their noses and complained about the stench, Olivia found an unconventional beauty in the threads of turquoise that swirled across the lake's surface like a Spirograph design. She snapped pictures of the zigzags the water bugs cut into the slime. One of those photos won a magazine contest, and when she moved back to Stillwater, she hung that picture in her house.

Her return was simple. She bought a place on Oak Street, got a job at the Peach Pit Stop gas station, and spent Friday nights in the bar. While all her old classmates chatted on Facebook about how stupid it was to stay, everyone at the High Bar talked about how stupid it was to leave. Sometimes she wondered about the life she might have lived in Minneapolis or New York, but when her toes squished into the lake's muddy bottom, she washed off the call of adventure with the comfort of home.

Tonight, as she walked into the water, she found no desire to be anywhere else.

"You should *totally* come," Mary said. She leaned up against the counter and tapped out another text message on her phone.

"I don't know," Olivia said, neatening a stack of lotto scratchers. Her job brought bouts of boredom; she obsessed over details to distract herself.

"Come on! It's going to be so much fun. It's going to be me, Mike, Sarah, and Kyle. We're just going to jump in the canoe and take it as far south as we can. We'll float all the way to the Gulf of Mexico if we want."

"How are you going to get back?"

"We've all chipped in a couple of hundred dollars. We'll sell the boat when we get down there. If we have enough money, we'll fly back or we'll buy an absolute beat-up clunker. We'll hitchhike back if we have to. Come on!"

"Where are you going to sleep, Huck Finn?"

Mary crossed her arms. "You're over thinking this."

"I really don't think so." Olivia swooped down and started to rearrange the candy display. She tottered, grabbed onto the counter, and waited for her vision to clear. Mary was starting to stress her out.

"It'll be a few weeks tops. Even if it completely sucks, you can put up with anything for a couple of weeks."

"No. I'm not going to piss away the rest of my summer avoiding getting hit by barges or drowning in locks or getting arrested for trespassing or getting kidnapped while I hitchhike home. Forget it."

"You are such a baby!"

Olivia clenched her fist and felt the tingles retreat to the palm

116

of her hand.

Mary narrowed her eyes at the motion. "What? Are you going to hit me?"

Despite herself, Olivia blushed. "No, but don't think the thought hasn't crossed my mind." She looked up from the candy and smiled.

"Come on. You have to live a little. Do this."

"What about Loony Days? You're going to miss Loony Days. You won't get the sportsman's club shirt, and I've got a picture of a loon on Stillwater that's going up for auction. You're going to miss seeing the lucky bidder. And the famous fire department Steak Out. Jeff makes the best ribs. You're really going to skip all that?"

"Yeah! And I bet we survive. We've done Loony Days for twenty-five years, Liv. Let's do something different. I'm sure Jeff will cook us ribs when we get back."

Olivia looked out the front door of the gas station. Heat waves rippled off the concrete. No wind disturbed the flag that hung on the house across the street. A perfect lake day. She imagined all the missed lake days, and that decided it.

"No," Olivia said. "I'm not leaving."

Mary threw up her hands. "Ugh. Fine." She spun around on her heels and walked out the door, almost knocking into Art Tanner.

Olivia felt like her hand was being electrocuted. Even her friends caused her stress these days. The tingling intensified and then receded to a dull sting.

The old farmer grunted at Mary's retreating figure. "What's her problem?" Art asked.

Olivia shrugged and went for the coffee pot. She didn't even need to ask. It was an 8 A.M. Sunday ritual, more regular in this town than church. Harry would show up next, then Dennis. She went to the far end of the counter and walked the pot back. Her hand shook under the weight. She didn't feel the smooth plastic handle slide through her hand, but she heard the glass shatter. The warm liquid soaked into her socks.

"Whoa!" Art said. He looked half annoyed, half amused.

Olivia's hand stayed frozen as if it were holding the pot.

"I think you can loosen that grip there, princess."

"No." She willed her fingers to move. "I can't." Her legs

117

wobbled, and the floor rushed toward her. Darkness followed.

The white ceiling was a blank canvas that loomed over Olivia. She forced herself to look away from it and focus on the doctor. His coat was as white and sterile as the ceiling.

"You have neurotoxicity poisoning," he said.

"Somebody's poisoning me?" Her brow crinkled as she tried to think of someone who would want her dead.

"I highly doubt it. It's more likely environmental. Drinking contaminated water. Working in close contact with pesticides or chemicals. Exposure to certain drugs." The doctor trailed off, gauging her reaction, looking for confirmation.

She scoffed and shook her head. She ran through a mental list, searching for the truth. After a pause that seemed too long, turquoise blooms bled into her vision. Her throat tightened. "What about swimming in contaminated waters?"

"Definitely."

She drew in a breath. "So what does that mean?"

The doctor looked down at his chart, then straight into her face. "There has been substantial exposure over a significant period of time. If we'd seen you sooner, there may have been a chance. Unfortunately, at this stage, there's nothing we can do. I'm sorry."

A tear ran its course down the side of her nose. She couldn't lift her hand to brush it away.

The words made no sense; they felt like a mockery—like the images that followed. She closed her eyes, searching for the thing she could ask for that would make this moment bearable. She saw a college campus and a canoe trip morph into a shot glass on the counter at the High Bar, a 40th anniversary Loony Days T-shirt, her friends gathered around a bonfire on the lake shore. The Mississippi river became a small lake. She envisioned a thin, gelatinous film across a body of water that had nowhere to run.

Behind closed eyes, all she could see were the still waters of home.

Poetry by Tim J. Brennan
My America (1969)

I need to write *my America*,
words about how the earth bears
everything, even crab apple trees,
the kind that grew on our corner lot
when I was twelve, spring
blossom showy, limb-filled
with white explosions,
thousands upon thousands
of white budding explosions,
sun stretched in the morning,
snapping dampness out of the air
like Mother used to snap
Father's wet shirts on cool mornings
from our back stoop before hanging them
crispy damp from our clothesline,
cedar-posted and sturdy, twenty feet
from our crab apple trees, the ones
which awed me when I was twelve.

Someday, I will press white blossoms
into a book and later read them
to my children so they can understand
my America in 1969, the one not talked
about in my white and thin history book.

Poetry by Ryan W. Keller
Burn Me

Do not keep grass or stone as mine.
I am neither holy nor hallowed.
I do not wish for rock
to bear my name.

I say pass to this rite.
Please, burn me.
Then spread the ashes
in amongst the trees.

Once I've drifted away,
take what's left
and give it away.
It no longer represents me.

Gather as friends for a good time.
Celebrate. Have a beer or some wine.
Toast to knowing you're the only thing
in this world that was ever mine.

Poetry by Sue Reed Crouse
Empty Nest

Before I knew it
I was the ghost
of a tree
naked limbs
heavy with snow
withered leaves
crisp with ice
my ringed heart had
begun its chemical
change
to a fissured
multi-hued
mineral
it had been the cadence
of her voice
that turned sunlight
to life
back in the days
when I had bark
burls and branches
and some warm creature
made in me
her home

Poetry by Gene R. Stark
Combine King

Dressed for his assent to the throne, green and yellow hat, with
                Carhartt brown,
Red-eyed frown, two days' face,
He assumes his place with dignity.
Enveloped with the exotic scent of diesel exhaust,
No cost is spared to speed him to his lengthy reign.
No disputes of royal lineage here
Surrounded by the withered leaves and stalks,
Frozen hulks that rattle a hollow bone-like cadence.
Length of reign determined by the fickle dews and frosts,
Production costs, and dockage loss.
To most he is the keeper of the food stocks,
Greatest gatherer in the kingdom.
To those below: his subject pheasant flocks and deer,
As he comes near, he's more the god of the second coming,
Hydraulics humming, like trumpets in the sky.

Fiction Honorable Mention by Paisley Kauffmann
Geraldine

Over her spectacles, Geraldine peeked up and down the aisle, lifted the seat of her rolling walker, and stashed a loaf of Wonder bread into its storage box. In the dairy aisle, she checked her list while waiting for a woman, ranting into her phone, to select a coffee creamer. The woman's young daughter watched Geraldine with a somber expression. Geraldine stuck her tongue out and crossed her eyes. The girl giggled and returned the gesture. Oblivious, the mother dropped her fancy flavored creamer into the cart and hurried off, whiplashing the child's neck. Geraldine opened the cooler and cold air temporarily fogged her glasses. She tucked a quart of milk into each of the hidden pockets she had sewn into her coat. This added two pounds to her already arthritic shoulders, but she figured it counted as weight-bearing exercise to help combat her osteoporosis. She scanned the aisle and slipped bologna into the American Heart Association bag hanging limply off the front of her walker. Opening a carton of Grade A organic free-range eggs, she checked for breakage before setting them on the walker's seat.

"Good day," Geraldine said to the man stocking shelves in the cracker and cookie aisle. He nodded, turned his back, and she stuffed a package of Oreos in her waistband.

"Ma'am," the man said. "Hold up."

Geraldine held her breath.

He approached her, holding out a piece of folded paper. "You dropped this."

"My grocery list. Thank you, son. I'd be lost without it."

As Geraldine approached an open checkout lane, a clerk with a nose ring and tattoos coloring her arms smiled. Geraldine gaped at the woman's staggered teeth, more fierce than any of her tattoos.

"Did you find everything okay?" the woman asked, swiping the eggs across the scanner.

"I did."

"One dollar and seventy-seven cents."

Geraldine opened her wallet exposing a few crumpled bills, and said, "Oh, dear."

The clerk shrugged politely.

Geraldine picked through the bills and said, "It's chilly in here, don't you think?"

The clerk glanced at her bare arms riddled in spider webs and skulls with red supple lips, and said, "I'm okay."

Handing her a five dollar bill, Geraldine watched the clerk snap it into the register before dropping her wallet on the conveyor belt. As if on cue, several coins clattered and rolled around.

"Oh, dear," Geraldine said.

The clerk helped collect her stray dimes and nickels.

"Thank you," Geraldine said.

"No problem. Three dollars and twenty-three cents is your change."

Geraldine pulled her hand back and said, "Where's the rest?"

The clerk paused before she looked at the register and said, "The eggs were a dollar seventy-seven and you gave me a five."

"No, sweetie, I gave you a ten."

"I'm sure you gave me a five. I punched five dollars into the register."

Geraldine opened her wallet, held it out for the clerk, and said, "I had a ten and now I don't. Should we get the manager over here?"

"Here." The clerk yanked the five from the register and added it to Geraldine's change.

"Thank you, dear. Have a lovely day."

The clerk didn't respond.

Geraldine left the frigid store and walked three blocks to George's house.

A trickle of sweat ran down the side of her face as she maneuvered her walker down the uneven cement path to George's front door. Through the screen she hollered, "George? Are you here?"

"Of course."

"Don't get up."

"I won't."

Holding the door open with her foot, she wrestled her walker across the threshold careful not to drop the eggs or lose the Oreos from her waistband. Her heart palpitated and she pressed her palm to her chest until it found a regular rhythm. George, reclined in front of the television, wore checkered golf pants and a striped sweater.

"I thought you went blind, not deaf," Geraldine said, plucking the remote from his hand and lowering the volume. "You're not going anywhere today or having visitors, are you?"

"No. Why? Don't I match?"

"You never match. Ready for some lunch?"

"I'm starving. Did you get bologna?"

"Plus a few other things," she said.

"Just take what I owe you from my wallet," George said. "You know where it is."

In the kitchen, Geraldine unloaded her coat and walker. She inspected a few suspicious items in his refrigerator before she set the milk and eggs on the shelf. Inside an empty box of frozen waffles, George's wallet was packed tight with cool crisp twenty dollar bills. Geraldine pulled out three, tucked them into her bra, and returned his wallet. She made two bologna sandwiches and carried the plates with a bag of Cheetos under her arm to the living room.

"Here you are," Geraldine said, placing the plate on his boney lap.

"Got it," he said, and tapped his fingers gingerly across the surface. "Are there chips?"

"Not yet." Geraldine shook the bag of Cheetos over his plate.

They ate in front of the television.

George licked his orange fingertips and Geraldine took the plates to the kitchen. She squeezed the last squirt of dish soap over the dirty dishes stacked in his sink.

"Do I have any Oreos?" George called to her.

"You do."

"Could you bring me three and a glass of milk?"

Geraldine opened the Oreos, filled George's cookie jar, and put the remainder in her bag. While he finished his cookies, she put clean sheets on his bed, fresh towels in his bathroom, and added dish soap to her shopping list.

"I'd be in a mess without you, Gerry. You're a good neighbor," he said as she was leaving.

"You were too, George," Geraldine said.

"But that was a long time ago."

"Regardless."

Geraldine pushed the walker down the street past the grocery store, to her apartment building. As she waited for the elevator, a young African girl wearing a turquoise garment, a *hijab* she would later learn, stood next to her. She had a cell phone tucked in the side of her *hijab* and spoke in a lyrical yet strident language. When the doors opened, Geraldine pushed her walker in and the girl followed. Geraldine noticed her beaded wallet sticking out the top of her purse. Watching the girl, she leaned forward, reached into her American Heart Association bag, and pulled out the Oreos.

"Want one?"

The girl, still speaking into her phone, smiled and shook her head.

Geraldine's fingertips pinched the fat wallet just as the doors opened and the girl glided out.

In her apartment, she filled the kettle and turned on the stove. The dented aluminum kettle reminded her of Herb, because he had always complained about the smell of her teas. She would never admit it aloud, but she was grateful to drink her Earl Grey in peace. Even his social security had been a disappointment.

Geraldine set the wallet, three twenties from her bra, and five dollar bill from the store on the table. As the kettle rattled, she eyed the brightly colored wallet carrying a mysteriously pleasant rose scent. She hoped it held at least fifty-four dollars, the rest of the cash she needed for her prescriptions. Her heart medication, already cut into half doses, would only last another five days. Every month, her prescriptions waited in white paper bags at the pharmacy while she purloined the money for their purchase. The whistling kettle startled her. She poured the water, curling with steam, into her mug and sat at the table dunking her teabag. With small silver tongs, she picked up a sugar cube from its bowl and dropped it into her tea. The sugar bowl was the last piece of her grandmother's Wedgwood Oberon collection; the rest had been sold to that sweaty man at the pawn shop. Slowly, she stirred her tea waiting for the cube to dissolve before she took a sip.

Geraldine turned the wallet over and unsnapped the closure. Inside was a photo of dark-skinned people, dressed similarly to the girl, posed arm and arm in front of a cement house. A skinny dog scratched at its ear next to the group. They smiled contagiously with broad white teeth and Geraldine involuntarily grinned back, but caught herself and shook her head. She pulled out a student identification card with the girl's radiant face. Her name was long and difficult to pronounce. According to the identification, she was a nursing student at the local community college. Unzipping a pocket, Geraldine inhaled sharply at the neatly tucked wad of green bills. She organized the money, totaling two hundred sixty-nine dollars, into discrete piles on the table. Geraldine added two twenties, a ten, and four ones to her own stack and returned the rest to the wallet.

On her formal stationary, Geraldine wrote the girl a note inquiring of her interest in a job helping an old blind man in the neighborhood. If so, Geraldine would quit buying her heart medication and make her final arrangements.

Poetry Honorable Mention by Jan Chronister
Hanging On

One of my students
writes about swinging
as a child, how
when she sits
in that hug
of rubber suspended
from ropes
she feels "sweet
happiness" again. She is
in her late teens
about as far from birth
as I am from death.

I remember that fullness
in my chest
last day of school
in June. On the cusp

of retirement
joy eludes me
found for a moment
in a cup of coffee
or glass of wine.

I am hanging on to that thread
in Stafford's poem, trying to
finish my life in clothes
I chose that morning
not some thin hospital gown.

I want to die satisfied
pulling weeds
threading needles
not tied up
with tubes in bed.

Creative Nonfiction by Kim A. Larson
Bus Number Seven

A freezing rain pelted the exterior of the bus that now rested in a field where clumps of black dirt peeked out amid patches of melting snow. We'd been tossed into each other's laps, but no one was injured—yet. On most days we'd come to expect worse jostling than this. We were like prisoners exiled to a primitive island in a test of survival of the fittest while riding Bus Number Seven.

Our driver staggered to the back of the school bus in search of injuries, instead of the usual contraband. "Is everyone all right?" He was a young man not much older than the high school seniors among us, which contributed to his inability to keep the older boys in line—and our bus on icy roads that spring afternoon.

After ensuring everyone's safety, the driver plodded back to his seat and attempted to drive us out. The engine revved and thick tires spun black dirt beneath us. Mud spewed everywhere as a blue-black smoke shrouded the stationary bus and increased the fear building in my heart. Would we ever get unstuck? How would I get home? As a third grader, these seemed valid questions.

Accepting his fate, the driver ambled to the back, where the cocks on the highest rungs of the pecking order roosted—the coveted back seats. I suspect even he trembled around this motley crew.

He addressed the boys in whose field we were stuck. "Your dad got a tractor?"

Of course he did. Their dad farmed like most of ours. Yet this foolish question wasn't met with the usual sarcasm, and the two boys followed the driver to the front. "Everybody stay put," he said. "We're going for help. We'll be right back." He closed the door behind them.

Be right back? How could they? This immensely long driveway privileged those boys to front-door delivery. Panic set in. It could be hours or days before they returned, and I knew what these restless natives were capable of.

One of the top-rung roosters crowed, "That was far out,

129

man!" Laughter broke out, releasing some of our tension. Then several boys tore up and down the aisle like sailors released on furlough. An older boy jumped into the driver's seat and started the bus. He probably thought he had more driving experience than our wet-behind-the-ears driver, and he very well may have. He floored the accelerator, and the bus rocked back and forth as he ground the gears.

After giving up, he relinquished control to the mob of boys ravaging the front, pulling and pushing knobs and buttons. At the hands of these trigger-happy hijackers, the rubber wipers screeched across the opaque windshield covered with ice. In the flurry of commotion, one of the boys toppled down the steps. Unscathed, he opened the now-at-eye-level cubbyhole and pulled out a dark green candle the size of a baseball.

The scent of pine wafted through the air near the front, where I sat fighting off tears. That same aroma had filled our kitchen months earlier when I had crafted candles to give as Christmas presents. For their mold I had used disposable inserts that fit snugly into plastic reusable Solo Cozy Cup holders. The makeshift mold narrowed like an upside down Christmas tree but had a flat, circular bottom the size of a half-dollar. The wick, tied around the middle of a pencil, had dangled like a fishing line in the center as the pencil rested on the lip of the disposable liner until the wax had cooled.

In the hands of these hoodlums, my gift was about to be used to play catch.

"Go for a bomb!" the boy up front shouted. He threw the scented candle at a boy running down the aisle to receive the pass. It hit him in the back of the head and he fell to his knees, moaning and holding his head. Another boy snatched it up as if it were a live grenade.

The boy up front yelled, "Throw it back, you douche bag!"

The wannabe rifled the candle to the front. Not as brave as he made himself out to be, the boy dodged the spiraling candle. It whizzed past his head and smacked the windshield, creating a spider web of cracks before dropping to the floor.

Everyone froze. The bus stopped rocking. A fearful silence

infused the air—as did the scent of retreat—and the stench of body odor. The boys scurried back to the rear of the bus, from where they exerted power and control.

One of the older boys hollered, "Nobody rats anybody out."

Was it this threat that blurred the names and faces of those that day? Or the forty-plus years that have since passed? I do remember, though, that a tractor finally pulled us back on the road and the bus driver delivered us home safely—for his last time.

Come to think of it, none of our drivers ever lasted more than one school year, if that. Who could blame them when the bus' faux leather seats would mysteriously start on fire? Or the emergency door alarm buzzed incessantly from tampering? I wonder how many pairs of underwear they'd heard ripping from the administration of snuggies. Or cries for help from those caught in headlocks receiving noogies. How many times had they cleaned bloody-nose splatters off the floor, seats, and windows at the end of the day?

No, I don't blame any of our drivers for not returning another year.

Unlike us, they'd had a choice.

Poetry by Kevin Zepper
Second Chance

Do you remember
that one time
when we tried
to pick up chicks
at the Second Chance Thrift Store?

It was a Friday afternoon,
nothing to do,
'cept smoke cigs,
and chug soda
right outta the bottle,
sitting on the curb,
scoping things out.

We walked in,
the bell jingled above us,
not one of the dozen odd
thrift chicks even looked.

It was a red tag sale,
stuff an old grocery bag
full of stuff
for a buck.

We were tagless guys,
from the bottom shelf,
and totally green.

Poetry by Patrick Cabello Hansel
Frank's Auto Repair

The dirtiest damn dog in the South Bronx lies in front of the best damn mechanic in the South Bronx. All the pastors go there. The dry drunk. The sex addict. The one whose church is about to crucify him. The one who can't stop throwing up at the altar during her first trimester. They all know Frank, and Frank does right by them. The dog lies right in the driveway you pull your piece-of-shit car into. Every bit of grease that was splashed around yesterday has landed on his coat. He takes no more breaths than are absolutely necessary. He is dirt and bereavement and luck rolled into one body. The dirtiest damn dog doesn't complain when you pull in, doesn't snap or refuse to move. He takes his time getting to his feet, shedding off the air that has coagulated around the dirt that has coagulated upon the grease upon his coat, turns and walks to a corner and lies down again. Frank always asks, "What do we have now?" He takes the key and he writes your number on a scrap of a big calendar two years old, and tells you he'll call you. If he can't fix it, it's on the house. I asked him once if the dog had a name, and he told me that it did, but for the life of him, he couldn't remember what it was.

Poetry by René Bartlett Montgomery
Voo Doo Chicken

This note is just to let you know
I have eaten your left-over pasta
that was partially hidden
behind the apple juice in the fridge.

You should hide it better next time.

You were probably
saving it for tomorrow's lunch
or perhaps an afternoon snack.

But you know Voo Doo Chicken
is my favorite
so forgive me.

It was so spicy
gooey delicious
I ate it all.

Creative Nonfiction by Laurie Fabrizio
Operation Rummage Sale

Dueling alarm clocks jolted me out of a sound slumber. Wiping the cobwebs from my eyes, I squinted to see the time. Hubby was still sporting his sleep apnea snorkel. The anaconda-sized hose coiled around his head. He was usually awake before me.

Donned in a hot-flash-resistant outfit, equipped with my steaming travel mug, I was armed and ready. Pointing my car toward Wayzata, I headed to the "mother of all church rummage sales." Operation Rummage Sale had commenced.

Stories had been swirling for weeks. The *Star Tribune* featured it as a front-page story. Local news media dispatched their reporters. I compiled a rummage sale checklist.

- Arrive early.
- Bring own bags.
- Be prepared to stand in line.
- Cell phone charged, ready to send photos to my daughters of any good deals.
- Cash and checkbook.
- Cheaters!!
- Consider camping out in parking lot the night before . . . Not!

Traffic was unusually light. An elderly gentleman flagged me into a parking spot. Grabbing my Trader Joe's bag, I braved the humidity and headed to the church. An hour early, and they were letting people in? Okay . . . it worked for me!

As I perused the aisles, my eyes darted from table to table. My sonar was in jewelry detection mode. Nothing but mangled pierced earrings. A vintage, gold-adorned Santa caught my attention. Two oval pictures for my bedroom beckoned me from across the room. Twenty-two dollars lighter in the wallet, I left wondering what all the hype was about.

Heading out of the parking lot, I glanced across the street. A golden aura surrounded an enormous church, as if it housed the Holy Grail. Two lines wrapped around the building like the Metrodome before a Packers-Vikings game. This was either a preview of the movie *Shades of Grey*, or I had gone to the wrong church.

"Oh crud!" I exclaimed. The realization washed over me like an ebbing tide. I had gone to the wrong sale. Scrambling, I rerouted in an attempt to nab a parking space. My elderly gentleman now directed me into an overgrown baseball field two blocks away.

Sprinting across the street, I fumbled to get my bag over my shoulder and prepared for battle. Two miles later, I grabbed a place in line. Clearly some people had camped out, their porta-tents strapped to their backs.

"Ding," chimed a bell.

"And they're off!" someone blared through a megaphone.

The line moved like a well-oiled machine. Flagging down a volunteer, I asked where I would find the jewelry. The anticipation was building. My heart was racing. I already dropped two pounds from the Tsunami hot flash that plagued me.

As I sprinted down the winding hallways, my eyes focused on the "Jewelry Room" sign at the end of the hall. Mecca!

Another line. People were being let in two or three people at a time. Are you kidding me? At this rate I would lose ten pounds. Fanning myself with the Trader Joe's bag, I noted shoppers carrying out lamps, heaping bags and other goodies.

Finally, it was my turn. I was soggy, caffeine-deprived and ready to rumble.

Reading glasses perched on my nose, paper plate in my hand, I glided from one side of the room to the other. Deftly, my hands worked in tandem, grabbing any interesting vintage jewelry along with bling.

"Wow!" exclaimed the cashier. "You found some great treasures." My paper plate spilled its contents all over the table.

Receipt in hand, I glanced at my watch. Got in, conquered, right on schedule. It was time to inspect the other rooms in search of vintage treasures. Several items caught my attention, but the prices were more that I wanted to spend. I scoped out the furniture tents, finding several items for my daughters' new homes. Snapping pictures, I texted them. No response. And they claim I don't respond to text messages!

Frustrated and tired, I grabbed my loot and headed home.

That evening, both daughters scolded me for not purchasing the pictured items.

"You never responded," I answered glibly. "Everything is 50% off tomorrow," slipped out of my mouth before I realized what I was saying.

"Mom, is there any way you could go tomorrow and pick up the . . ."

Was I crazy? My brain was warped by continuous hot flashes. Perhaps my mind was corroded by mold from too many estate sales.

"I'll try," I sighed, avoiding commitment. Mom guilt slowly set in.

The next morning I swore I was in the movie *Ground Hog Day*. Dueling alarms awoke me. Fresh clothes, and coffee . . . I felt like Bill Murray.

My first stop was the furniture tent. A young woman passed me carrying the chair my daughter wanted. Not a good sign. Cruising through, I noted that everything on my list was gone. This time, I scolded myself for not getting up earlier.

The sign for jewelry signaled me. My pulse quickened. Fifty percent off! No lines. No waiting.

Paper plate in hand, I discovered more great finds. Pieces I had overlooked the day before beckoned me. Placing my heaping plate by the chatty cashier, I helped expedite my checkout.

Invigorated, I once again perused the other rooms. I snatched up the treasures that piqued my interest the day before. A wooden baby grand piano that opens up to reveal a bar set . . . awesome! China vanity set from the 1940s: matching powder and cream jars, hair receiver and matching tray. Even a German filigree alarm clock from the 1950s was nestled under a shelf. Dusty, wonderful treasures, purchased at half price.

Mission accomplished. My arms ached as I lugged my purchases out the door. Passing a couple of tents for sale, I hesitated for a moment. Hmm . . . could give me an edge for next year's sale.

Waving to Bill Murray, I headed to my car. A few tweaks to my rummage sale check list and I would be good to go.

- Portable battery operated fan. Check!
- Go to correct rummage sale. Check, check, check!

* * *

Poetry by Joanne Morén
Fickle Fog

Fog's wraithlike fingers
slowly, seductively, caress
Lake's silky surface.

Whispering softly,
Fog lingers
but a moment;

then rises,
deserts Lake,
to dissolve
into Sun's warm embrace.

Poetry by Janice Larson Braun
Aeolus

Perhaps it is boredom
That causes the wind,
Restlessly pacing for days,
To gather itself
And spring into the sky with a roar.

It toys with the lake,
Lifting, dropping, rolling—
Hurling great sheets of water to splinter against the rocks
And dissolve into bits of foam.

Then it leaps up the hill between the stricken trees,
Flattening the grass,
And explodes at the crest with wild frenzy.

Gentler trees bend at the waist
And let their spines take the force of it.
But the young Norway pines cluster together,
Jostling each other with loud shouts,
Reveling in unleashed power—
Anxious for their turn to rule the world.

Poetry by *Thadra Sheridan*
Short, Fat Marilyn Monroe

On Halloween,
I dressed up as
Marilyn Monroe.
I wanted a chance
to wear that
long red velvet dress
I bought in New York.
I dropped 40 bucks
on a curly blonde wig
and spent an hour on my make-up.
I wanted to feel sexy.
And it was working for a while,
I guess.
I spent the whole night at work
fielding catcalls with
men ogling my breasts,
showcased strategically in a
strapless push-up bra.
But he crumpled my
paper sex-esteem
with one flip remark about
a model on TV, who,
no offense,
had a much nicer ass than me.
And I drove home
feeling like a
short, fat girl
in a tight, red dress
and a wig that was too blonde
for Marilyn Monroe.

Poetry by Marlys Guimaraes
If You Knew Me

You would know I live where
the only sound heard at five below
zero is the squeaking of boots on snow,

that I am like French Bread, crusty, soft
in the middle, and easily devoured,

that it's February and I keep forgetting to bag
the dried oregano from last summer's garden
hanging on living room curtain rods,
shriveled like ancient kelp,

that I miss the smell of freshly mimeographed
paper.

Did I say I have long ago quit using the
treadmill sitting in my living room,
but you know that, don't you?

That I once thought I had lice
but didn't,

that I hoard paper, especially if they have
words on them,

that to relieve tension, I wander around
Ace Hardware or Fleet Farm,
touching tools and orange
cords while lusting after miraculous remedies for
the broken things in life.

> > >

If I were a car, I'd be a yellow
Volkswagen bug in need of new tires and a tune up,

that my patchwork quilt of religion
has some empty blocks and is sewn
with easy-release running stitches

and yes, I would thoroughly enjoy accessing
your veins or irrigating an open
oozing wound, if you wanted me to,

that the best day of my life was the day
my daughter was born, and it wasn't
because of the birthing process and

that I don't like guns, but if you seduce my husband, I will shoot you.

Creative Nonfiction by Beth Diane Bradley
Talking About My Generation

Accidents happen. I know this for a fact because I am one. Meaning my existence was not planned, at least not by my parents. My family not only had the normal generation gap between parents and children, but we had a second one of 12 years between my siblings and me.

For the most part, it created a useful and interesting dynamic. My sister and brother acted as understudies to my real parents, who were still recovering from the first time around. This meant I got to be an honorary teenager at two years old. My diaper-clad rendition of the twist was unmatched by any other toddler in the neighborhood.

I loved to play dress up in my sister's prom dresses. I waddled around in her high heels, imagining they were Cinderella's glass slippers, and smeared her lipstick all over my face. I found the fact that she shaved her legs to be extremely glamorous—sadly, shaving my own legs has never been quite as fascinating.

I was six when my sister got married, and my parents gave me the standard line that I wasn't losing my sister, I was gaining a brother. In my little girl mind, that meant he was moving in with us. When I found out that was not the case, it led to serious abandonment issues—which has given me a convenient excuse for any problems I've had ever since.

The generation gap grew when I became a real teenager. My parents had to adjust from my sister, who wore poodle skirts, to me and my blue jeans. I remember my mother gazing with horror at my ragged bell bottom jeans and saying, "Denim pants are for milking cows in the barn. We do not live on a farm!"

In my later teens, I learned it was often best to protect my parents from the harsh realities of my generation. I made sure some of my activities were as invisible as those cows we didn't have. That tactic worked fine until one of my friends spilled peppermint schnapps on the basement rug.

Years later I became a mother of teenagers, and the generation gap between us was measured in megabytes. My oldest son was especially adept at outsmarting his parents at a very young age. We put parental controls on our computer and safely guarded the password, but it didn't take long before he learned how to undo anything that cramped his style. Like with most parents of our era, the kids ended up teaching us how to use our cell phones, fix our computers, and navigate the latest online trends.

Each generation has its own slang, and that is groovy, neat or cool—depending on your age, man—which reminds me about the time my oldest son had some friends over to our house. I was talking to his brother on the phone, explaining to him some girls had left their thongs by the door, and went down to the basement. He said, with a touch of sarcasm, he couldn't wait to come home and check that out.

Duh. My bad! When my kids were learning how to talk, I didn't realize some day they'd teach me the proper name for a pair of shoes. Now that's what I call a flip-flop.

Poetry by Audrey Kletscher Helbling
Winter Centerfolds

Winter exposes, uncovers, strips,
drops Autumn's dress upon the land,
fallen leaves caressing bare ankles.

Leafless trees accentuate thin limbs
like leggy Twiggy models
swaying along the runway of the sky.

Gravel roads tease,
lead wandering eyes to linger
on voluptuous farm sites.

Barns flash lipstick red.
Silos stand erect.
Farmhouses vanish in virgin white.

This is Winter. Disrobed. Revealed.
Alluring in her nakedness,
only pages away from Temptress Spring.

Poetry by Thomas C. Stetzler
Stick Man's Blues

I am one of long dangling arms,
feet that don't reach the ground.
I am all wooden thoughts,
rough edges, clumsy words,
awkward silences.
Strangers pass quickly,
avert their gazes.
Friends embrace reluctantly,
walk away with slivers.

Poetry by Jennifer Hernandez
In Fog, Driving

Enveloped in diaphanous haze
moving forward almost blindly
from indistinct pearly whorls
suddenly morph solid shapes.
In an instant, reality altered.
Sometimes   a warning:
pinpricks of headlights
where before   nothing.

Is this how thoughts form?
Dreams?
From the muzzy jumble
swirling neurological soup
appear those high beams
or the flicker of a match
signals that orient   or disorient
clarify   or muddy.

For how can we tell in the fog
which path is the right one?
Is the beacon friendly or deceiving?
That buzzing violet glow of
St. Elmo's fire   a promise that
the storm will soon abate?
Or a lantern fish whose luminescence
lures prey to a hasty end?

My inner compass urges me onward.
Can I trust it?
Or is it, too, confused by the fog?

Poetry by Susan Niemela Vollmer
Awake at One A.M.

Hot and restless in the August night
I wander out to lie on the couch
hoping to catch a breath of the east wind
through the slats in the blinds

Along with the soothing breeze
come the night sounds
the rumble of the factories near the river
trucks humming along the highway

Bass thrums from a car radio
as the young man across the street
swoops into his driveway
after closing down the bars

The night owl neighbor
drags and thumps her garbage cans
across the concrete
ready for morning pick up

From the lake a loon calls
the pure notes rise and hold
then slide down to disappear
like a silent dive deep into the dark lake

Creative Nonfiction Honorable Mention
by Charmaine Pappas Donovan
Go Gentle, Dad, into that Good Night

Do Not Go Gentle into That Good Night was written by Dylan Thomas in 1952, my
birth year. He wrote this poem during the final illness of his father who was a
grammar school teacher.

Each day goes slower since Dad's stroke. I always know where to find him. Not like when he resided in Heartwood Assisted Living. Back then I visited twice a week and sometimes missed seeing him while I washed his clothes or straightened his apartment. That felt good because I knew he was socializing with friends. Now in a nursing home, he is either at meals or in bed. Last April an early morning call dragged me from my bed. An ER doctor told me that Dad had had a hemorrhagic stroke. He said Dad was awake, alert and able to speak. "I'll come right over," I said, taking a deep breath. "He must be scared."

A stroke. Although Dad took medication for high blood pressure, this was not something I anticipated. I thought of my friend Ruth. Her father was wheelchair-bound due to a stroke but, in his case, he had trouble speaking. I pondered when Dad began receiving medications from the staff because he was confused about what pills to take and when to take them.

He lay on a stretcher, the sound of the heart monitor steady and loud. "Oh, Dad," I said. "How are you?" He took my hand in his right hand, gripping it. "I'm okay," he said with a slur. The next several days were unpredictable. His blood pressure ran high, but the doctors said it was best that way. This would help circulation in the brain where blood had pooled. There was a chance he could develop seizures. Because of the paralysis on the left side of his body, his ability to swallow was compromised. He couldn't eat and at first received only intravenous fluids. Dad had a living will and did not plan to be kept alive by artificial means. He never wanted dialysis if his polycystic kidney disease progressed. He would accept only IV fluids and antibiotics. No feeding tube.

If Dad was not able to swallow, hospice would be the next step. By the sixth day, Dad began eating yogurt and pudding with special coaching. He was able to drink honey-thick liquids. Two days later Medicare said he was ready to go to a rehabilitation facility. He was transferred by Medi-Van while I drove ahead so I would be at Bethany when the van arrived. He was placed in an unoccupied double room. Relieved that a nurse on Station Five was someone I knew, I begged her to watch over Dad. I sat in the parking lot and cried; afraid he would not make it through the night. When I visited the next day he was working with a new coach to help improve his swallowing.

When he first went to the nursing home for rehab, I was optimistic that Dad would walk again. He had been athletic, strutting up and down the halls of Heartwood while other elderlies tooled around with their walkers and electric carts. Dad's interest in physical therapy waned as the workouts became harder and more painful. He didn't like the way occupational and physical therapists wheeled him to the other side of the facility at odd hours. He was a retired teacher who organized his day by the clock. The randomness of the workouts irritated him. He was confused about the purpose of the therapies.

Because Dad's brain bleed was on the right side, plus in the back of his brain, he also lost half of his eyesight. He can't see the call button for the nurse, so he presses a flat button when he needs help. He has a condition called left-side neglect. Holding up his limp left arm with his good right hand, he'll say, "This isn't mine, you know. Someone took my arm and stuck me with this statue." I remind him he had a stroke and that the paralyzed arm and leg are still his. Although his eyes see perfectly according to the eye doctor, his brain only allows him to see the image on the right side of each eye. These images converge to form an odd, spliced picture. Once during dinner he said, "There's a coffin in my room." After his meal, I wheeled him back to his room where we looked at an empty bed. I patted the bed and said, "Dad, this is a bed. But if you only saw half of it, it might look like a coffin." This satisfied him.

Since Dad's stroke he weighs forty pounds less and recently started hospice. Chewing is a chore. A bedsore—caused by an ill-fitting wheelchair—broke open again recently, so he is back on bedrest except for meals. His life is as narrow as he is thin. I can no longer cajole him into eating. I spend time each day visiting this slip of a man, yet I see that Dad's tether to this earth is as flimsy as a trail of smoke. While still hospitalized for the stroke, he once told me, "I wish I would have died. I wanted to join your mother."

Today I am filled with a dread all children must feel when they realize they must love their parent enough to let him or her go. When the hospice chaplain urged me to talk to Dad—a man who was always spooky about death—about his funeral arrangements, I realized that I must trust Dad's decision to let go of his life one bite at a time. As a coach and teacher, he has done much to enrich others; I don't want to impose on his right to die with the dignity he so much deserves. Though I may "rage, rage against the dying" of his light in my life, I pray he goes gentle into that eternal good night.

Poetry by Mary Willette Hughes
Finding Signs

On our street last night, below twin Basswood trees,
    a flashy-red sports car. Golden leaves had drifted
down and down, layering up and up on the hood,
    the roof, front and back windows . . . an undeniable
sign the season of Autumn cannot, and will not stop.

This morning the car waits for its middle-aged owner
    to brush the leaves away before driving. But he
doesn't. He sits in the car, revs the motor and lays
    a long dark patch. Leaves fly. He speeds away to
the highway; whitewall tires screech at the stop sign.

If only signs of old age could be wind-swept away
    as easily as leaves and find a bright red car below,
maybe a Mazda Miata, waiting to zoom our last days.
    But . . . no! In bold, black letters a sign shouts:
DEAD END. We try to brake. We cannot stop.

Creative Nonfiction by Kit Rohrbach
Love at Eleven

It was the summer after fifth grade when I found Damon Runyon in the attic. He was in a box back under the eaves, turning brown at the edges, smelling of dust and old paper. For three school's-out months I went through the usual motions: swam at the municipal pool, screeched through clarinet lessons, cheered my brother's baseball games. But every time no one was looking I was in the attic, hiding from well-meaning adults who would shoo me out into the fresh air for my own good. I was in the attic with Harry the Horse, Spanish John, and Little Isadore.

I didn't take them with me when I went back to Logan Valley Elementary in September. They are not such guys as would fit in in a grade school classroom, and I wanted to be too old for imaginary friends. I wrote my "How I Spent the Summer" essay about perfecting my cannon ball off the diving board and a family trip to the Jersey shore. On through the winter I diagrammed sentences, found the lowest common denominator, and memorized the dates of Civil War battles. I went to a dance wearing a new pink dress with a rose on the collar and never thought of Miss Dream Street Rose or Good Time Charley.

Years later, out of school, out of college, in a used book store, I found Damon Runyon again. This time I knew him better. I knew he'd been a newspaper reporter and a gambler, a promoter of baseball, horse racing, and roller derby. I knew he died on the day I was born and Eddie Rickenbacker scattered his ashes from a plane over Broadway. I knew that somewhere in an early story, he'd once used a contraction.

I still haven't found it. I get so caught up in the affairs of guys and dolls I forget to notice. But I keep looking.

Poetry by Marlys Guimaraes
Blessed Assurance

Suppose you believed your mother, so
you took the kitchen knife, the one used

for chopping zucchini and green onions
and sliced open the seam of your lover's

pillow, kissed a delicate swan's feather,
placed it deep, to mingle with the down

of unfamiliar geese, then replaced
the slashed seam with intricate stitches,

pricking your ring finger to leave a scarlet
drop on the white pillowcase, as you

repeated, *he loves me, he loves me not.*
Imagine if the last stitch ended

on *he loves me not.* Then would you
believe your mother—that a swan's

feather sewn into his pillow
would ensure fidelity?

And what if she was wrong?

Creative Nonfiction by Jesse Birnstihl
Identity

When I was in ninth grade, Mr. Renzaglia taught me the word *melancholy*. It instantly resonated with me, becoming one of my favorite words. Although its denotation indicates a prolonged state of sadness, I heard only the musicality of the syllables. What a delicious sound: not only sad, but also beautiful.

That same year, the nameless health teacher taught me the word *depression*. The ugliness of this word was glaring, so I tried it on in secret. I realized it fit, but I didn't tell anyone for years. Instead, I wore it like long underwear, close to my skin and out of sight of the world. I'm sure a few people caught a glimpse of it here and there, but I would *never* admit to it.

Some secrets are too painful to share.

Depression wasn't the only ugly word I tried on. I heard it on the playground, I think, when I was in fifth or sixth grade. Not understanding, I went home and looked it up in the *Merriam-Webster* dictionary while my mom and dad were on a walk.

Homosexual: sexually attracted to people of the same sex.

Actually, that is the definition as it appears now, in 2015, in the *Merriam-Webster* online dictionary. The definition I remember is crueler, and certainly one I couldn't imagine attaching to myself.

I never understood why people were mean to me—why they called me names, pushed me, punched me. I mean, I understood why they didn't want me on their team for kickball, but I didn't understand why I deserved to be hated. Maybe it's that I was an easy target—that my mom and the Bible said *turn the other cheek*. Mostly, I tried to run.

I've been running ever since.

Mental illnesses run on both sides of my family. My dad's youngest brother killed himself. My mom's youngest brother has suffered from a debilitating depression for at least ten years.

In high school, I considered myself depressed, but I would never have admitted to it. To do so would be to admit weakness—something I could not do as someone who faced constant bullying. So I feigned normalcy as best I could.

I went through the daily routine of school, which I would have enjoyed if not for the students. People always ask me why I don't go to my class reunions. It has been fifteen years now and I still have no desire to see more than a small handful of my classmates.

Yes, academics were easy for me; socializing was difficult. I didn't know how to talk with others. I didn't like sports, didn't understand them. So I buried myself in books and video games and seclusion.

Choir helped, and French. I made friends in mock trial and knowledge bowl, in the school musical and the chess club and even the Bible club. But there was always a part of me that stood just outside of every group, that wouldn't let me truly get close to other people. It was the part of me that wanted to die.

I wanted to kill myself.

I didn't figure out I was a homosexual until I was 19 and in college. I should have figured it out before that, as I'm sure most people had, but perhaps I wasn't gay yet, or wasn't ready to deal with the ramifications of being gay. I'm really not sure.

The word homosexual seemed so oppressive and foreign that it couldn't possibly describe me. At least, that's what I told myself. I liked girls. I liked girls a lot. They didn't like me, but I loved girls. I had a secret crush on a different girl just about every year. Despite my longing for a girlfriend, I should have recognized the signs that I was attracted to males as well. The first clear memory is this:

Seventh grade. I am in gym class. We are in a basketball unit. The teacher has assigned us to teams for 3 on 3 games. I am terrified; everyone knows I am not good at anything in gym class. One of my teammates passes the ball to me even though he knows I can't do anything with it. I do something, pass it back maybe, or shoot. It doesn't matter. What matters is

156

that he doesn't make fun of me, that he says something kind to me.

In this moment, I come to revere him. I begin to think about him often; I want desperately to be his friend, although I have no idea how. I don't understand that I love him, that his red hair and freckles will be permanently etched in my mind's eye.

Some truths are too painful to admit.

As an adult, I consider myself, more or less, normal. I have a job that I enjoy (most of the time) and that pays the bills. I don't want to kill myself most of the time. I'm generally pretty happy. Or I pretend to be.

I feign happiness in the way I once feigned normalcy. I'm not entirely sure what it feels like, in the way that someone who has never been in love might understand the concept, but not the intensity, of the actual emotion.

One of my students called me out on it once. Nik, who is more of a son than a student to me, told me I wasn't happy. "Of course I am," I lied.

"You're so full of it." His tone was that of someone who knows he is right. Proud. Mocking.

"OK," I indulged him. "What makes you think I'm not happy?"

"Because you smile with your mouth, not your eyes," he said. And in that moment, we understood each other.

I may never understand what it means to be happy, but at least I finally understand what it means to be human. It's a life filled with moments of kindness, painful truths, and melancholy memories that reveal our souls with startling clarity.

Poetry Honorable Mention by Stephanie Brown
Bone

The couple drives along, leisure in their pockets,
two months before summer's swell of crowds.

They've become part of the plein-air scene
Riccoboni paints—*Beach on Coronado Island.*

The Silver Strand current ferries in mica. Thousands
of tiny, glittering gold mirrors, cast onto her lover's

bare feet, reflecting the face of a younger
self animated with curiosity. He calls to her

and points to a white object half in the dune.
She gently tugs and discovers a bone.

She rotates it around, rubs her thumb over
flecks of mica clinging to its sponge-like ends,

finds the perfect heart in the bone's center.
Look at this! she exclaims. A passing glance

is all he affords: *Why would you save something
like* that? His disgust triggers an undertow of shame.

She watches him seize the artist's brush, dip it in matte
black, paints over her pastel paradise. The slate

blue sky disappears, then the gulls. He ridicules her
and there go the rocks, the shoreline, the glitter.

His mocking continues and she feels herself
shrink as she walks toward the bruised reef,

the bone, a pale shadow, her back painted black.

Poetry by Nancy Hengeveld
Under the Ozone

We are breathing the same air the dinosaurs breathed,
drinking the same water.

This air was breathed by rain forests,
Buddha,
Christ.

When I dive to a reef,
the air I breathe from my tank,
exhale through a regulator,
bubbles up,
bursts at the surface.
Whales breathe it.
You breathe it.
I breathe it again.

The sea evaporates into clouds,
rains,
snows,
melts,
soaks into the earth,
where the bones of dinosaurs wait.

We are warming our bodies.
We are burning their bones.

We are breathing the same air the dinosaurs breathed,
drinking the same water.

Once it is gone,
it is gone.

There is no more.

Poetry by Mim Kagol
I-29 North to Grand Forks

On our way to a wedding,
this long June twilight spreading wide
around us,

Driving the compass needle,
paralleling the border,
barreling north
through the easy darkening,

Up the map through the flattest land,
feeling our left-side eyes, our
left-side shoulders glow golden
as the massive sun fills the car,
fills the west,

Slipping off the edge of Earth
beneath a rising horizon,

But so, so reluctantly slowly
it seems less a loss than a promise,
a vow to be here again and again
forever.

Poetry by Niomi Rohn Phillips
The Ocean's Gifts

Heat shivers arms and shoulders
as I emerge from the sheltering shade
of the cliff trail onto the beach.
Hawaiians call it *chicken skin.*

I search for sea glass and shells
in the solitude
of a cove
far from the sunbathers.

Cool washes over my ankles
at water's edge
where waves roll over a reef
with rhythmic roar.

I gasp with childlike surprise—
midst the rocks and coral washing up on shore
a cowrie unscathed by sea salt
a perfect pink and brown shell

> sensual sun, symphony of waves
> rough gravel on the soles of my feet
> at shoreline
> sinking footsteps in the sand
> of the infinite beach beyond

I will package this day
to unwrap
when Winter
finds me in another place.

Poetry by Larry Schug
Approaching Sharon Springs

Driving through Kansas at two a.m.,
everyone in the van asleep but me,
hands on the steering wheel, eyes on the road,
and the Grateful Dead, jamming "Dark Star,"
time and space becoming irrelevant.
Across the expanse of the Great Plains,
Sharon Springs is just another minor sun
called a star after dark by the inhabitants
of a trivial planet of rock,
lonely as a cork floating in the sea,
despite the illusion we've chosen to embrace
in order to make sense of our being
in this particular anywhere, anywhen;
of being at all.

Creative Nonfiction Honorable Mention
by Eric Chandler
Buckle Up

I worked for NASA. Sure, it was just an internship at the Ames Research Laboratory near San Francisco. But "I work for NASA" is good at cocktail parties. Now, I know you really want to hear about aeronautical engineering, but instead, I'm going to tell you how I got to California that summer.

My truck was a black, two-door pickup. A 1986 GMC S-15 with a standard transmission. It had a red interior and a red vinyl bench seat that comfortably sat two people. Three if you were desperate. You cranked the window down with a handle. No headrests. No airbags. No air conditioning. I described it as, "Four cylinders of raw power."

On my first trip across the continent, I bought a little charm to hang from the rear view mirror. It was a little medallion in the shape of New Hampshire, my birthplace. Over the next 15 years, I drove that truck across the country several times. Like a criminal. I sped everywhere. Rules were for the little people.

Like most good road trips, this story involves the great American West and a woman. She was a redhead. Fiery and opinionated, just like you'd expect. She was an old high school friend, and she joined me for my trip to California. I was 20 and searching for the girl I'd spend eternity with. Or, at least, the next couple of weeks.

When I invited my friend to drive across country, like most young men, I thought we could be more than friends. I drove faster than the speed limit. But, I always wore my seat belt. (That paradox escaped me at the time.) I asked my companion to put on her seat belt when we started. She refused. I said her face would go through the windshield if we hit something. She wouldn't budge. Naturally, I allowed this transgression since, you know, I wanted to be more than friends.

We drove west out of Utah on Highway 50. Two lanes of desolation. We rocketed through the desert with the radio blasting to compete with the roaring wind. The road traveled in a straight line across the flats. It was eerie how the pavement went to the vanishing point at the foot of the next mountain range. We arrived at the spine of rock and the road snaked over the height of land. We descended the other side and the road snapped straight again like a chalk line. We repeated this cycle of cruising and climbing for several hours.

We learned why the highway is called "the loneliest road in America." We rarely saw another car. My foot got heavier and heavier. We entered a strange landscape of sand near Fallon, Nevada. We rounded a dune and saw the cop. The rollers started flashing. I lifted off the accelerator and pulled over.

The policeman showed up at my window in stereotypical fashion. Flat brimmed hat. Mirrored sunglasses. Crisp pressed shirt. Shiny badge. The whole deal.

"Do you know how fast you were going?" he asked.

I didn't have a problem telling the truth. The problem was the speedometer. When he caught me, the needle was all the way to the right against the little pin. It only went to 85.

I said, "85?"

"I had you going 93," he said. "The speed limit is 55." He took my license and registration back to the cruiser.

Deep down, I was surprised and pleased my little four-banger could even go that fast. I don't remember what we talked about while we waited or if we even talked at all. I remember the sand was bright in the sun. The dunes towered over us as I waited for him to come back and let me off with a warning.

The officer strolled back up to the truck and held out the ticket. "I wrote you up for going 89 in a 55. If I actually said you were going over 90, you'd spend the night here in jail."

I thought: *Did he just say jail? Because it sounded like he just said jail.*

"If you'd like to contest this, you can show up in court on

this date. Or you can pay the fine."

I looked at the paper in my hand, which was trembling a little bit, and it said $120. "Thank you very much, officer." I hoped he could see how grateful I was not to visit the crowbar hotel.

But, it wasn't over. He leaned down and looked over at the redhead. "And you, young lady. I assume you were wearing a seat belt when I pulled this young man over." He just had to turn over the only rock that had monsters under it.

I looked to my right with horror. What was she going to say?

She said, "No. I. Wasn't." Well, she wasn't a liar.

I don't know what the cop saw. What I saw was her red hair and the red interior of the truck and the red vinyl seat all bursting into flame. I turned my shocked face to the policeman. He swiveled his head to look at me. I could see my open mouth in his sunglasses.

"I'm pretty sure she was. Don't you think?" he said.

"Yes, sir. I'm pretty sure she was."

We kept looking at each other for a second. Then he shook his head and walked back to his cruiser. I cranked up the truck and pulled back onto the road.

Years later, I took that little black truck to Korea. While I was there, I invited a woman to go on a road trip to a Buddhist temple in the mountains. She and I have a different pickup truck now. It's a mid-size four-door that holds our kids. It's the second car I've ever owned. I drive slower. Everybody but the dog wears a seat belt. The tiny New Hampshire still hangs off the rear view mirror. And, strangely enough, the truck is red.

Poetry by Niomi Rohn Phillips
String of Pearls

after five decades
            he still moves
left
                  me right
vying for position and power

                  but

      when we dance
      our moves are smooth

                  face to face
                  arms overhead
                  open hands touching
                  feet in sync

                  we
      glide left

                        glide right

                  fingertips
                        meet
                  midst twirl
                  for direction
      turn left
                        turn right

                  bodies and brains
                  in harmony

            romance renewed
            with Glenn Miller

166

Poetry by Marilyn Wolff
You Can't Choose Who You Love

You can't choose who you love
because if you did,
wouldn't you have chosen the boy next door
with the puppy dog eyes
who thought you were the best thing since mustard?
Who grew up to own the corner bank
and who still looks at you,
after all these years,
like all he wants to do for the rest of his life
is curl up in your lap and gaze at your face?

Would you really choose the
cowboy who rode into town
one Saturday night to steer you onto the dance floor
and leave two days later with your heart?
Who loved your innocence and your laughter
so much that he took it with him when he left?
Whose life didn't fit in any way with yours,
but whose body fit perfectly?
And how in the quiet of the night
he is the one you think about and want to hold.

Not the lapdog.
Never the lapdog.

Poetry by Scharlie Martin
Icy Dilemma

You might think me rude.
It's not that I don't want to be
Your friend. I do.
It's more like my new occupation
Entails just staring out the window
Like a statue frozen in time.
At least that's what it looks like
I'm doing.
Actually, I'm busy trying to calculate
A way out of this frozen labyrinth
That is me.
It's like my voice is perpetually frozen—
A wooly mammoth in a self-contained iceberg
No matter how hard I strain
I remain contained within the
Walls of my untimely affliction.

Poor sad soul!
If I could just squeak out
A little mouse voice
I could crack the ice
And get you to
Love me.

Fiction by Adrian S. Potter
Brandy and Merlot

May I have a glass of merlot, please?"

"Pardon me?" I asked.

"May I have a glass of merlot, please?" she repeated.

I was astonished. My dog had never before voiced a single word in English, let alone formed a complete sentence. So I did the only thing I could do; I got her a glass of merlot. I politely placed the wine on the floor in front of her. She stood over the glass, lowered her mouth and muzzle into it, and began to drink deliberately. I kept watching her, my mouth wide open.

"Apologies, but I can't hold a glass in a proper manner. No fingers or opposable thumbs," she said, after noticing I was still staring.

I shook my head, attempting to recalibrate my thoughts, and said, "No. I've seen you drink from a glass before. Not a wine glass, but a glass nonetheless. I'm just amazed you're talking to me."

"Well, that's a secret. In fact, I probably could have my canine card revoked for speaking in front of a human."

"You have a canine card?"

"No," she said, shaking her head. "I was speaking figuratively."

"Oh. But you could get in trouble?"

"Not trouble . . . just shunned, by strays and other neighborhood dogs . . ."

"Oh. Well, then why are you talking to me?"

She sat down and, ignoring her merlot, looked straight at me. I could have sworn I heard a slight sigh.

"I have to tell you something," she began. "We need to talk."

"Perhaps you don't know this, from not talking to people and all, but good conversations rarely begin with those words," I said, feigning a synthetic smile.

Shaking her head, she turned back to her merlot. She dipped

her mouth in and lapped up some more wine. Then she looked towards me. I waited impatiently to hear what was on her mind.

"Look, it's over. I'm sorry."

"What?" I asked, perplexed.

Then she started a familiar soliloquy I've heard from females before, just not a female of her species. "It's not you. It's me. I can't continue on like this. I need something more. You have your friends, your hobbies, and your career. And I'm not saying there's anything wrong with that. There isn't. But all I have is you. I define myself by you. I'm not really Brandy. I'm Craig's dog. That was enough for a while. But now I need more. I have to find my identity."

She gazed down at the red wine, not drinking it, just contemplating it. I was stunned, to say the least. Never before had Brandy uttered a word. And now, she opened her mouth and verbally heaped a mountain of discontent upon me.

"So, that's it," I said. "You're leaving. You've already made up your mind. And there's nothing I can say or do to change it, huh?"

"No."

"Well, where will you go?"

"It's complicated."

"What the hell does that mean?"

"Craig," she said, sheepishly looking down at the merlot and then back up at me. "There's somebody else. You have to believe me. I didn't plan for it to happen this way."

Now I was pissed. Before I was cordial, subconsciously thinking she might return to my doorstep soon enough after a taste of freedom. But Brandy had already hooked up with another owner behind my back. That was an indignation I could not accept.

"Fine! Leave! But don't think you're taking anything with you. I loved you, Brandy! I took care of you. And you went and found someone else! Get out of here, then. But don't even think about taking that Italian leather collar. That's mine!"

I stood up, removed the fancy collar and ID tags from her neck, and opened the front door. And the bitch walked out of my life forever.

Poetry by Cheryl Weibye Wilke
Autumn In the City

A dog's bark sounds different
in the fall. It carries the dusty
color of crimson through back alleys
leading from a crosstown
neighborhood. It wanders hungry
alongside the prairie waves
of an afternoon breeze. It comes
at about the time a sharp
and faraway whistle freezes
thirty maroon-and-gold boys
on the high school football field.
It awakens the smell of raked
leaves burning in the backyard
barrel ricocheted by rust and holes.
Like the rustle of stalks
in departed gardens, a dog's bark
in the fall echoes the melancholy, middle-aged
spirit of all falls past. Really, the dog is
long gone, but its bark rings
forth someone's small town calling.

Poetry by Janice Larson Braun
The Keeper of Hope

Sitting on the cold steel table
While strange fingers probe and needles sting,
Her eyes lock on mine,
Watching for a sign, a cue,
To tell her whether or not to let the fear in.
I am the one.

I am the keeper of all things—
 of the treats on the counter
 of the rules against jumping and biting and barking.
I am the keeper of the peace
 when the fuzzy little kitty stretches, yawns,
 and transforms into a yellow-eyed demon with claws.
I keep her safe—
 from skunks and cars and wood ticks
 and now, from cancerous tumors on the spleen.

But mostly I am the keeper of the heart.
And so, as I turn out the light
And we snuggle deeply into our pillows
And synchronize our breathing,
We slip into the night ahead
Together.

Creative Nonfiction by Gene R. Stark
A Pup at the Door

The puppy was displaying his usual antics. What does one expect from a twenty-week old pup? Of course he'd been chewing on everything. The frayed table leg displayed his handiwork. A ragged bunch of puppy-toys lay scattered on the rug.

My older dog lay in drowsy contentment by the couch. His perfect discipline and calm demeanor, such obvious contrast with the raw and raucous behavior of the pup. We had endured the little delinquent puppy for yet another evening. Sometimes the brash stupidity of a pup is overwhelming.

Relief from the rigors of raising a pup was imminent as I let the little fur-ball outside in preparation for kenneling him up in his dog-box for the night. Thank goodness he was at least at the age where he'd sleep through the night and allow us and our older dog a night's rest and relief from his exuberance.

The pup stuck his nose into the cold night air. With unusual calm he placed his silky paws onto the deck. A mellow sense of intention overtook the little dog. He surveyed the night with an intense display of purpose. A few steps out onto the deck, he sat and surveyed a dark world, filled with all the terrors that every dog knows are out there. His nose trembled as he turned his head to catch every nuance of scent in each direction.

For a moment he was no longer a pup. Then I realized that somehow he knew. In some mysterious way the puppy realized that he would be part of a canine succession, a taking of the responsibility for the abode of Man. This would be his cave to protect, his fire to stand beside against all the invaders and perils of the night.

The moment passed and he leaped off the deck to pursue a dried leaf in the yard. The older dog came to my side and looked at the frolicking pup; he also knew.

Poetry by Kate Halverson
Show—Don't Tell

my never quite getting how
one does one without the other

Their deep voices said it all as they grunted
their way across the ice toward their fish house.

Did I do both? Show with my words
or tell too much or little?

Writer's disease—over-analyzing
every sound bite, flippant dogmas

not easy to explain in black and white,
heavy hitting do's and do nots

rarely telling the story clear enough
to show the one and only way to go.

Frustrated, over-analyzing the teacher's
retort, she crunched up her paper and threw

it in the brass wastepaper basket less than five
feet away while her classmates scrolled

through messages on their iPhones
oblivious to her turmoil.

Fiction by Jerry Mevissen
Witness

I'll be glad when this call is over. The Lord is demanding a lot of me today." Jacob checked his watch, then placed a rubber band around an *Awake* and *Watchtower* pamphlet. "Maybe she won't be home."

Isaiah held both hands to the wheel of the old Dodge station wagon and steered it down the long gravel drive. "She's always been home ever since I started the mission."

"Maybe she won't want to discuss her version of the Bible. Maybe she'll be fixing supper. Maybe she'll take pity on us."

"The Lord will ask no more than you can deliver."

The sky to the west shone blazing red, rebutting a gray November landscape of stark black trees and a dusting of snow. A light shone through the window of the house ahead and smoke swirled from the chimney. A shaggy Newfoundland dog waggled out to meet the car.

"She's home," Isaiah said. He parked in front of the garage and turned off the ignition. Doffing his hat and bowing his head, he folded his hands. "Lord, that we may expand Thy kingdom."

"In His name we pray." Jacob lifted his head and reached for his briefcase. "Let's go."

"Five o'clock, and it's dark already," Jacob said on the walk to the door. "I told Arlene I'd be home by 5:30."

"The Lord's work is our top priority," Isaiah said as he knocked.

Mrs. Harvey opened the door. "I knew you were coming," she said. "The neighbors have an alert system. Two men in a car, both wearing neckties? How many people up and down the road answered the door?"

"The Lord's word will find a way," Isaiah said, handing her the pamphlets.

"Who is it, Gladys?" A man's voice wheezed from a

backroom.

"The Jehovah's Witnesses."

"Tell them we don't want any."

"You were here about a month ago and left pamphlets," Mrs. Harvey said. "I've been waiting to ask you a few questions."

Isaiah leaned forward. Jacob sneaked a look at his watch.

"About *the one true faith*," Mrs. Harvey said. "You believe that you found it, right?"

"Oh, yes." Isaiah nodded his head. "If mine wasn't the one true faith, I'd search for it."

"But if it's the one true faith for you, is it the one true faith for the rest of the world?"

"Yes, yes. God's truth is absolute. It is our mission to bring you the truth."

"You won't run out of prospects then," Mrs. Harvey said. "You may have a problem convincing all the Jews and Muslims and Hindus and Buddhists, not to mention your fellow Christians. But tell me about the Bible. You interpret it as the absolute word of God, right? Immutable and infallible for all time, correct?"

"Yes, the Bible." Isaiah reached in the pocket of his coat and retrieved a small book. He patted it and held it to his heart. "Everything we need to know is here."

"And a few things we don't need to know. Slavery, for example. And human sacrifice. Doesn't the Old Testament condone that?"

Isaiah looked at Jacob. Jacob looked at his hands. "I haven't read the Hebrew text," Isaiah said. "Sometimes passages suffer in translation." He reached into his briefcase. "You might be interested in this." He handed her a copy of *What Does the Bible Really Teach?*

"I'll look at it, but I don't expect to find those answers. Another question. I notice that you are strong believers in Creationism. Doesn't science disprove much of what is written in the Bible? Do you believe in the seven-day creation cycle? Adam and Eve? The Garden of Eden?"

"With all my heart and soul," Isaiah said. "A beautiful story of God's might and beneficence, and man's ingratitude and weakness."

"Do you see it as metaphor or fact?"

"Fact, ma'am. It's all spelled out there in the book." He slid a finger around his shirt collar and felt sweat building under his arms.

"You might be thinking about how your story will play when forms of life are discovered in other galaxies. But enough for today." She smiled. "Excuse me a second."

She walked to the kitchen and returned with a plastic bag of cookies. "Thanks so much for talking to me. Or letting me talk to you. My everyday conversations are limited to 'Did you take your pills?' or 'Should I turn down the heat?' or 'Should I turn up the volume?' I haven't talked ideas for years."

"Charity is its own reward," Isaiah said, reaching for the cookies. "I hope you find answers to your searching in that book. Or the Bible." He opened the door.

Outside, Jacob petted the dog on the walk. "It's times like this I wish I was a drinking man."

Isaiah wiped his hand across his brow. "We're not that far from the Broken Hart Bar."

Poetry by Doris Lueth Stengel
For the Son who Never Has Poems
Written About Him

He is the eldest, lives nearest,
the one who comes when help is needed.
Even as a child he was fair-minded.
He cut candy bars for his siblings
using a ruler to be sure pieces were equal.

Close enough for emergencies,
for the unglamorous jobs,
he gets "parent duty."
As they age, they are a yoke
around his neck, yet
this child and his children
know them best:
share ballgames, fishing,
concerts, holidays.

A man of faith, he understands
it is the prodigal
returning from a far country
who receives the robe and feast.
Yet would this son
who "stayed home"
trade the years of learning
at his father's elbow,
trade the meals at his mother's table?

There are things more satisfying
than feast or poetry.

Fiction by Gene R. Stark
The Bridge at the Confluence

It was December of 1925. We were pouring concrete in some of the worst weather I can remember ever working concrete. The sky was spitting pellets of some sort of frozen water across the emerging structure. I looked across the wide valley of the Minnesota River from my lofty vantage point. We had begun in the spring and the colors of green had merged to flaming fall, until now only a hazy black and white picture remained.

I was working for Koss Construction Company out of Des Moines, Iowa. They had won the bid to build the reinforced concrete arch bridge which was to span the Minnesota River Valley between Mendota and Fort Snelling. I worked the whole job from 1924 to the finish in 1926.

The weather in the winter of 1925 shut us down from December 22 until March 3. The days in December were very hard, even dangerous as the temperatures went down to ten degrees below zero. The wind was relentless up on the bridge and the brunt of the cruel season engulfed us and punished us as we entered the season of white.

The bridge was to be a link, tying the deep fertile soils and expansive prairie to the south with the pine forests and mines in the north. The worlds seemed to meet here where the Minnesota River flowed into the Mississippi. A lot of us workers met here as well. It took a huge number of laborers to complete such a historically large project.

Jack was drawn here for the same reasons we all were. The pay was good and it was steady work, assured for at least two years. So I remember that day, as we were seemingly pasted to the slate-gray sky, aboard the methodical crossing of the valley. I looked down on the ferry, operating some of its last runs before the freeze-up.

We were making the crossing in a final, steady march across the river. Ours was the crossing of crossings. We paved the way for

179

thousands to make the crossing more easily and more effortlessly than ever before. We were drawn to the far embankment to the north, not by an architect's plan, but by the ageless need to meet, to bring worlds together.

I worked at finishing concrete on that day. Jack got called to help with a big pour of concrete on the next arch. I had gotten to know Jack in the way that you get to know men who work at tough jobs. We would have a smoke, and talk about the foremen. "The foreman on the pouring crew is a real slave-driver." Jack breathed out a cloud of smoke and condensed breath.

"I've heard there's no slacking out there," I agreed.

Jack was a bright kid, could do a day's work, always ready to pitch in. I figured he would do well, maybe be kept on by Koss for other jobs.

The cold day in December is the last day I saw Jack. I asked about him the next day. Two other laborers just shook their heads and turned away. I only heard the rumors. Some said he slipped, others that he was hit. The concrete flowed and he was gone. There wasn't a trace of him and even now I know he is part of the eternal crossing, lost here, yet monumentalized into a part of the ageless pursuit of the other side.

Construction stopped on the twenty-second and men were laid off. Crews changed the next spring in the usual seasonal flux of construction workers. I never heard anything official about Jack and I had never found out enough about him to make any further connections.

Maybe it's because of Jack that I'm here today at the bridge dedication. God knows I've seen enough of it, crossed its concrete expanse, smelled its endless tons of green concrete, and witnessed its steel entrails placed into their eternally arched bodies. Yet, I'm drawn back to the crossing.

The day is much like the day in December when Jack vanished into the project. The day is cold and snow lays upon the bridge railings and the valley below is cloaked in winter. It's Monday,

180

November 8, 1926, and the bridge is to be officially opened.

I have helped build the bridge, and now all the bodies and bones of the ages cry out to me in anguish and excitement. We and those before us have been drawn here to live and die, strive and love, and march into the communion of the ages.

I drive across the newly completed Mendota Bridge in honor and respect, because I knew him and I worked with him here. Although I hardly knew him, Jack was a friend.

The rhetoric cries to the heavens, as the ancient cries of ice and water mingle with the concrete-covered bones. I hear the accolades spoken by Governor Christianson, the politician's praise of those who risked their lives to complete the bridge. I hear no mention of Jack or any of us who labored to cross the valley.

Governor Christianson cuts the golden rope to open the bridge. The rhetoric and acclaim of the elected civil servants pervade the festive atmosphere, cut the frigid grasp of the November day. The words fall upon my ears as the flakes of snow descend and swirl into the cold wind. Yet the words lead me away, deaden the crystal days of construction and open my thoughts to the ages. Today thousands make the crossing and their spirits mingle with those who have crossed and those who will cross. We all set our sights upon the confluence, the meeting of the ages. Soon my ears leave the sounds of history in the making and my mind focuses upon the history already made. The thought of Jack in perpetual crossing turns my gaze to the clouds and there I see a form new to my intellect. An eagle soars in a break in the clouds, headed to the meeting of time and place, gliding to the eternal convergence, ultimately to alight upon the high wooded ridge which oversees the coming-together of life and death.

Poetry by Richard Fenton Sederstrom
Fall Harvest

My dock will be out until the first sowing of winter.
Then Ben and the boys will bring it to shore, a harvest,
section by section. Free the shore to ancient time.

Then the lake will be open to winter, shore empty
of human traffic. We will see deer drinking on shore
and now and then a stag with his randy rack of antlers.

The leaves will all have fallen, save for those of a few
recalcitrant oaks, trees always the last to loose their
grip of labor. The forest will have opened for winter.

Long-dead aspen will reappear, lying as always
with their heads, shorn of rotted tree-tops, all facing sunrise.
I will turn and face the sunset. Sunset is the drive back

to the desert where we face the subtler and sadder
fall, a slight twinge of cool *deja vu* to mark the season.
Closer each fall, in joy I face sunset, toward harvest.

Creative Nonfiction by Cindy Fox
River Voices

 T he annual tubing down the Otter Tail River. Heat, deer flies, sand, and dirt. Family and friends buzz in my cabin and fly out with suntan lotion, bug spray, and can coolers. I debate if I should go or not, weighing common sense against nonsense. The sun is no longer my friend, the shade a cool place to hide my scars and spider veins. I envision a tipsy prankster flipping my tube over and my body sinking like a heavy anchor. No thanks. Hard for me to get in and out of my easy chair, much less an inner tube that doesn't touch the ground. I need to feel the earth below my feet. I bow out from the annual river run, hold my ground amid relentless protests. "Come on, Cindy! One more time!"

The farm kids bring tractor tubes that sprout valve stems, which poke your thighs and remind you of their past lives. In the garage, the compressor roars as my son fills their inner tubes. Others listen for hisses, slow leaks that will leave them dog paddling in the river's raging undercurrent. Holes are patched, silly names painted on their stretched skins: DRUNKEN SAILOR, FLOAT MY BOAT, RIVER RAT, SWEET PEA, BEAVER SNATCHER, and others not PG-rated. My old tube, QUEEN BEE, lays crumpled on the "Go-to-the-Dump" pile. Her life deflated, too many patches to make her a trusty vessel in the murky waters where fallen trees lurk below the surface.

The city visitors clutch their store-bought tubes that look like comfy chairs with headrests and drink holders in their arms. No gaudy names mar their vinyl veneers splashed with blue and white, hot pink, and neon orange. Even camo for the floater who chooses to float disguised, usually an avid hunter. And, of course, the "must have" tubes, specially designed to hold family-sized coolers filled with beverages.

The flotation devices are piled high in the pickup box. Greasy bodies sit on the tailgate, ensuring no tubes will fly onto the gravel road. I drive my passengers two miles up the road. The fellows fling the tubes and they smack the water like doughnuts sizzling in hot grease.

Tubers wade in and hoot as the river envelopes their ankles, thighs, torsos. They dunk themselves, screaming with sheer joy and shock of the cold water. Timid ones are splashed and screech bloody murder. Everyone scrambles to lay on their backs with hind-ends in the water. Goose bumps melt as the sun kisses their faces, chests and legs, and the hot rubber heats the backs of their thighs and necks. My three young grandsons wear life jackets that bob around their faces, all aglow with the excitement of their first river run. They wave. "Bye, Grandma. See ya later!" I wave back and watch the caravan drift away on their slow float down the river.

Their voices skip over the water, then sink like fallen stones as they round the river bend. I turn to go, but decide to linger awhile. I dip my toes into the water, then step in and gasp when the sharp chill swirls around my ankles and calves. The river has sucked me in and, for a moment, I feel myself drifting backwards in time.

My body was hard and beautiful. Fearless, I rode high on the waves of adventure and ignored NO TRESPASSING signs. My hands braided around the neighbor's rope swing, I ran free and wild like Tarzan's woman, and leaped into the river. My hair raked the river bottom into a cloud of silt. I spiraled up, tan and glistening, a fountain of youth I thought would last forever.

I hear distant wails of laughter drunk on fun and sun, the gulp of bodies plunging into the river. I know the river well, know they've floated to the second loop in the river that meanders slow and lazy. I envision my eldest son climbing on the leafless tree that arches its back over the water. I imagine myself there as a tree looking down and a tree that has fallen, though its roots still cling to the riverbank. Alive and almost gone. I picture his arms outstretched sailing through the warm August air, then folding around his knees as he plummets into the deep river pocket. The *kaploosh* is like a rush reeling me over to that young woman who jumped into her life headfirst.

Trickles of chatter fade downstream while I come down from

184

a high, like silt settling on the river bottom. For a long, timeless moment, I wait for the river to speak to me. I hear the whisper of the late afternoon breeze running its fingers over the cattails. I close my eyes and sense my body swaying. I hear the river lapping and gurgling, feel its perennial flow embracing my legs, soothing and eternal. The voices of the river, past and present, calm me. I inhale deeply and smell the earthy scent of moist soil. I feel the pull of the earth below my feet as I wade back to shore. Puffs of silt rise and then fall, leaving only a shadow of a footprint for the evening that follows.

Poetry by John Harrington
Winter Rivers

Winter rivers need watching. They often play hide and seek, shapeshift from water to ice to mist to dreams. Take count of deep cold, cloudy days. They may deceive you into believing you can walk on water. To learn the truth you must be brave enough, crazy enough to discover yourself. From the bank, watch a northwest wind drift fallen snow across the leading edge of snow-dunes. See meanders form across the ice. Their shapes wisp into ghosts of Summer's wavelets. Islands appear, disappear, reappear, float in mist, drift on the surface. Go, traipse a magic landscape frozen solid as glass. Your first steps onto river's ceiling create no crack, cause no splash, no surprise. Take another, and the next . . . Each one holds you—in suspense. Would you do this if local mountains had peaks worth climbing?

The Origins of The Talking Stick

The talking stick is a Native American tradition used to facilitate an orderly discussion. The stick is made of wood, decorated with feathers or fur, beads or paint, or a combination of all. Usually speakers are arranged in a talking circle and the stick is passed from hand to hand as the discussion progresses. It encourages all to speak and allows each person to speak without interruption. The talking stick brings all natural elements together to guide and direct the talking circle. —Anne Dunn

This year, we received nearly 300 submissions from 143 writers. The Editorial Board selected 89 poems, 19 creative nonfiction and 15 fiction pieces from 95 writers for inclusion in this volume. Please submit again!

www.thetalkingstick.com
www.jackpinewriters.com

Contributors 2014

*(Without the following contributors, this Talking Stick would
not have been possible! Thank you to everyone!)*

Benefactors
Louise Bottrell
Marlys Guimaraes
Sonja Kosler
Mike Lein
Harlan and Marlene Stoehr

Special Friends/Singles
Cindy Fox
Linda Maki

Good Friends/Couples
Ed and Genell Poitras

Friends/Couple
Sandra Clough
Lorelei Erdmann

Good Friends/Single
Joan Dreyer
Kristin Johnson
Margaret M. Marty
Susan McMillan
Susan Perala-Dewey
Bonnie West

Friends/Single
Chet Corey
Charmaine Pappas Donovan
Barbara Draper
Jeanne A. Everhart
Jean and Greg Mevissen
Ronald j. Palmer

Author List

Angela Ahlgren
Lina Belar
James L. Bettendorf
Jesse Birnstihl
Nicole Borg
Beth Diane Bradley
Janice Larson Braun
Tim J. Brennan
Stephanie Brown
Eric Chandler
Jan Chronister
Mary A. Conrad
Chet Corey
Sue Reed Crouse
Frances Ann Crowley
Charmaine Pappas Donovan
Larry Ellingson
Jeanne A. Everhart
Laurie Fabrizio
Cindy Fox
Annaliese Gehres
Georgia A. Greeley
Marlys Guimaraes
Kate Halverson
Patrick Cabello Hansel
Laura L. Hansen
Paula L. Hari
John Harrington
Sharon Harris
Audrey Kletscher Helbling
Nancy Hengeveld
Jennifer Hernandez
Sandra Howlett
Mary Willette Hughes
Rhoda Jackson
Arnie Johanson
Mary Jones
Mim Kagol
Meridel Kahl
Paisley Kauffmann
Ryan W. Keller
Kathryn Knudson
Susan Koefod
Sonja Kosler
Kim A. Larson
Kristin Laurel
Mike Lein

Kathleen Lindstrom
Linda Maki
Cheyenne Marco
Scharlie Martin
Margaret M. Marty
Michael McCormick
Susan McMillan
Jerry Mevissen
René Bartlett Montgomery
Joanne Morén
Anne Morgan
Ryan M. Neely
Patricia Nelsen
David Eric Northington
Ronald j. Palmer
Kathleen J. Pettit
Niomi Rohn Phillips
Shasha C. Porter
Adrian S. Potter
Al Rieper
Kit Rohrbach
Deb Schlueter
Mary Schmidt
Larry Schug
Richard Fenton Sederstrom
Thadra Sheridan
Gene R. Stark
Peter William Stein
Doris Lueth Stengel
Thomas C. Stetzler
Scott Stewart
Marlene Mattila Stoehr
Annie Stopyro
Janet Thompson
Joseph E. Tietge
Peggy Trojan
Ruth Jesness Tweed
William Upjohn
Steven R. Vogel
Susan Niemela Vollmer
Justin Watkins
Bonnie West
Andrea Westby
Cheryl Weibye Wilke
Marilyn Wolff
Tarah L. Wolff
Kevin Zepper